HIDDEN AMERICA

HIDDEN AMERICA

by *Roland Wells Robbins*
and Evan Jones

ALFRED · A · KNOPF   *NEW YORK*

1966

L. C. Catalog card number: 59-9257

© *Roland W. Robbins and Evan Jones, 1959*

THIS IS A BORZOI BOOK, PUBLISHED BY ALFRED A. KNOPF, INC.

SECOND PRINTING, NOVEMBER 1962

THIRD PRINTING, DECEMBER 1966

To THE MEN WHO DID THE DIGGING —

*without whose help this book could not
have been written*

Foreword

ALTHOUGH the first person is used repeatedly, this book is less an autobiography than it is a story of archaeology in which one man's part provides a unifying theme. Yet this is the work of two writers—a collaboration resulting from my encounter with Evan Jones in 1952. The interest he showed then in my excavation of the Saugus Ironworks site has continued through the years. He has spent many days with me as I have worked at other digs, and that time together has made possible the story which follows.

No man's work is ever wholly independent. Every archaeologist today is constantly making use of the discoveries and the methods developed by those who preceded him. So it is with this book as it attempts to map the frontiers in American archaeology. We are indebted to the many who have described their excavations in both popular and technical publications, and particularly to those in the nineteenth century who worked so valiantly to awaken interest in the American history that had so speedily been buried. Perhaps this book can help to spur more interest, and to show more Americans the genuine excitement to be found in digging.

ROLAND WELLS ROBBINS

Lincoln, Massachusetts, 1959

Contents

CONTENTS

List of Illustrations

List of Illustrations

List of Illustrations

List of Illustrations

HIDDEN AMERICA

1

Under This Earth

THE RIVANNA RIVER flows to join the James through the red soil of Piedmont Virginia, and forms a gentle artery in this fertile valley. The terrain is attractive and ideal for agriculture, and people have thrived in the valley since long before the dawn of history. White men had been here for one hundred and fifty years when, one eighteenth-century summer day, Thomas Jefferson turned his restless, searching mind to the inhabitants who had preceded him on the Rivanna's banks. From the hill on which he had built Monticello he had often looked down upon the site of an Indian village, with its clearly evident burial mound. And when a lull came in his political life he found the time to investigate. He opened the mound and compiled notes so well conceived that archaeologists now think of him as "our first scientific digger."

Like hundreds before and since, Jefferson was an amateur. His distinction lay in the fact that his quest was for knowledge instead of loot. In an era when men were digging at Pompeii and Herculaneum with no greater purpose than to recover articles of artistic or monetary value, digging without caution, digging without recording a single detail of their findings—in this era Jefferson excavated an Indian burial mound simply to learn more about the aborigines whose history was lost in the mists of time.

Still, in Jefferson's curiosity there was nothing new. Some of the Pilgrims were amateur archaeologists. As early as 1622, in a book published in London, the excavation of an Indian grave at Truro on Cape Cod was described. "We mused what it should be," the report says, "and resolved to dig it up." The diggers found a hunter's bow, a knife, a packneedle, "two or three old iron things," bowls, trays, dishes, "and such like things." Perhaps the most interesting objects of all in this discovery so soon after the voyage of the *Mayflower* were "a sailor's canvass cassock and a pair of cloth breeches." The dead Indian, it developed, had been buried with European clothing taken from the crew of a French ship that had been wrecked off the cape in 1616.

America has piqued the curiosity of those with an archaeological urge since the very beginning. Mystery cloaked the land when our forebears arrived. Indian trails wound through the tall, thick forests that stretched from the Atlantic to the Mississippi. Giant temple mounds rose, barren, secret, unexplored, on plateaus in the southeast, the middle west. Cliff dwellings were found abandoned. Other Indians were here to greet the Pilgrims, the Jamestown settlers, the Spanish, the voyageurs from France, yet these natives knew nothing of the vanished ones, the builders of temples, the ceramic artists of the Mimbres River. Vikings had been here too. How many others?

Curiosity about such things was shunted aside as the new Americans kept themselves busy building a new nation faster than any had been built before. New mysteries were created as the settlers established villages and abandoned them, threw up cities on the sites of towns. As the continent was tamed, as highways, railways, oil and power lines scarred the land, the old—which was really so very new—was buried as irreparably as Pompeii had been. Too busy to examine the mystery of the Indians, Americans were creating their own past and systematically burying it in the ground.

It is only in the last quarter century that diggers have begun to search the earth for a closer look at the changes in America made by white men. The digging done in the nineteenth century, what little there was of it, was aimed, as was Jefferson's, at the vestiges of the Red Man. Such men as Ephraim George Squier, a New York journalist, were pioneers in surveying, sketching, and digging into sepulchral, religious, and defensive earthworks; in the 1840's Squier compiled the first extensive catalogue of mounds, including such startling, enormous earthen replicas as the Great Serpent in Ohio (1,348 feet long with an open jaw that extends across seventy-five feet of prairie), and the mounds shaped like buffalo, panthers, lynx, and other animals in Wisconsin. First knowledge of the archaeological treasures of the southwest came in 1874 when William Henry Jackson photographed the cliff dwellings in Colorado's Mancos River canyon, not far from Mesa Verde. A half-dozen years later Adolph Bandelier undertook the first scientific explorations in the southwest.

Yet virtually no one had mustered interest in the archaeology of early European settlements until a group in New York led by William L. Calver and Reginald Pelham Bolton in the late nineteenth century began to excavate Colonial and Revolutionary War sites in the vicinity of Manhattan. Bolton and Calver were active for more than thirty years. Their digs revealed the sites of five Revolutionary encampments—they dug into what had been the James Gordon Bennett estate and found bushels of military arti-

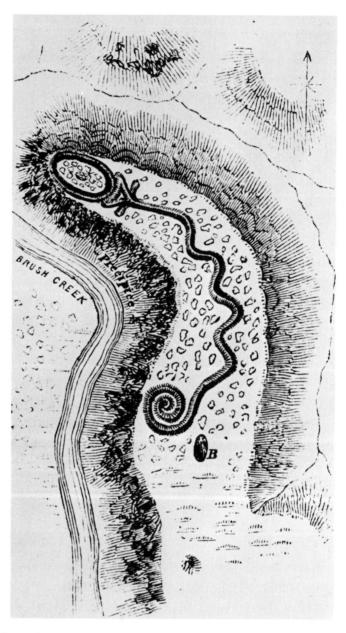

Great Serpent Mound in Adams County, Ohio, as drawn by a nineteenth-century illustrator.

facts left by the British in their siege of Fort Washington in 1776.

The Bolton-Calver committee, in the course of hundreds of weekends in the dirt, dug at Fort George, at Fort Ticonderoga, at West Point, and Fort Haldiman on the St. Lawrence River. The thousands of relics they unearthed, tokens of the battles which did more to forge the American character than those of any other war, are now a part of the New-York Historical Society Museum collections. "Each object," says Richard J. Koke, the Museum's curator, "contributes to the picture of military life, and in the collection are also found coins, ceramics, glassware, rum bottles, shovels, nails, spikes, camp axes, tent-pin butts, Dutch tile fragments, keys, scissors, pothooks, spoons, knives, forks, a canteen, ice creepers, bale seals, lead pencils, an apothecary's weight, stirrups, bridle bits, horse and ox shoes, and even strips of lead which were sewn into the lining of uniforms to keep them in shape."

These scientific explorations of American history were completed none too soon, Koke says. "Where once was located the defenses of Fort George on Laurel Hill stands the George Washington High School. The sites of the Holland's Ferry camp and the camps of the 17th Regiment of Foot, the Musketeer Regiment von Donop, the Body Regiment, and the Hessian cantonment along Bennett Avenue have all been obliterated by real estate and industrial development." On farms where Bolton and Calver "found many mementoes of the Colonial and Revolutionary occupations, now spread the repair and storage yards of the Independent Subway. Of the many earthworks which were visible when the committee members first started their archaeological investigations only the American Redoubt in Fort Washington Park remains today."

In spite of this urgency, Bolton and Calver had few successors. Few diggers thought to invest their energy in probing a civilization so like their own. Few felt the lure of the seventeenth and eight-

Under This Earth

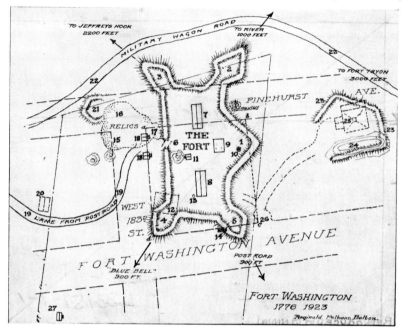

Three metropolitan streets now cut through site of Revolutionary War fortifications in Manhattan. The map is by Reginald Pelham Bolton, pioneer historic-sites archaeologist.

eenth centuries—either in Europe or America. The romance of archaeology remained linked to peoples who had lived in a vague era called antiquity. All this was natural enough. Excavations in the Mediterranean area brought forth civilizations which time had completely forgotten. Discoveries of the cave paintings at Altamira and Lascaux illuminated the culture of men whose only tools were made of stone. An aura of glamour surrounded Old World archaeology, and still does.

The inevitable interest of Americans in archaeology as a counterpart to their own history was slow in coming. But in the 1930's several excavations along the eastern seaboard gave hints of the rich archaeological treasure underground. The dig at Jamestown

HIDDEN AMERICA

8

Island in 1934 proved more exciting and fruitful than the most optimistic had anticipated. Discoveries at Williamsburg stirred even greater interest among thousands of Americans. The work of diggers was helping to form a new conception of the culture of the earliest English colonies in the New World.

The impress on the public consciousness began to be felt. In 1935 Congress passed the Historic Sites Act, a bill designed to bring about the preservation of prehistoric and historic objects, monuments, buildings, and sites, whether they were on Federal land or not. The National Park Service was authorized to implement the program. Out of the legislation came the vast Inter-Agency Archaeological Program for the salvage of scientific data

Workshop site at Jamestown was found buried in a woods on the edge of Pitch and Tar Swamp. National Park Service archaeologists believe the structure to have been either a seventeenth-century brewhouse, bakery or distillery.

The most impressive foundation unearthed at Jamestown is this 160 by 20 foot row house containing a cellar and a giant fireplace at the east end, and four other fireplaces in the four main divisions. Six families may have lived in this seventeenth-century prototype of Baltimore and Philadelphia row houses.

from sites to be flooded by the construction of hundreds of government dams. In addition, working funds and active interest came from such private individuals as John D. Rockefeller, Jr., who made the Williamburg restoration possible. At this Virginia project almost four hundred buildings have been reconstructed on the origal foundations uncovered by archaeologists. "The town," according to Ivor Noel Hume, Williamsburg's chief archaeologist, "is as close to being a living eighteenth-century city as the twentieth century will permit."

Archaeologists also have been studying the French and Spanish efforts at colonization; they have thrown new light on the era of expansion along the Missouri and in the west and northwest. At last it has become apparent that there are archaeological opportunities throughout the United States. In fact, so numerous are these opportunities that there are not enough fully trained scientists to explore them all, and many important discoveries of the future will be made by amateurs who are willing to absorb sufficient training to properly implement their curiosity.

It was curiosity about my own community that led me to dig in Massachusetts when I had no more equipment than a shovel and a questioning mind. At the time I had a thriving business as a house painter and handy man—and no archaeological training whatsoever. But I found that simple tools and the rudiments of a scientific approach, cautiously exercised, could ferret out history that had evaded others; and, as time passed, the opportunities to

Colonial Williamsburg archaeologists found the foundations of the historic Raleigh Tavern soon after excavations began. The hostelry was a famous meeting place before and during the Revolutionary War, and is believed to have been erected prior to 1739.

The original basement walls of Williamsburg's Governor's Palace were found largely intact, along with a floor of massive stones.

do so became so demanding that I ceased to be an expert at washing other people's windows and renovating other people's houses, and was established as a working archaeologist.

Yet before I was moved to use a digging-tool of any kind, I had been unwittingly preparing myself. It was in the spring of 1942, while perched on a stepladder painting the living-room of a Concord home, that I was drawn into a discussion which was to lead me eventually to archaeology. In those war years Daniel Chester French's statue of the Minute Man, erected at Concord's Old North Bridge—"where once the embattled farmers stood and fired the shot heard round the world"—was being reproduced everywhere as the emblem of America's victory effort. The war had magnified the fame of the sculptured Minute Man, but facts about its origin had been obscured, and there were many impromptu debates staged by Concord citizens. I doubt that anyone ever was less prepared to act as a historical arbiter, but I felt over-

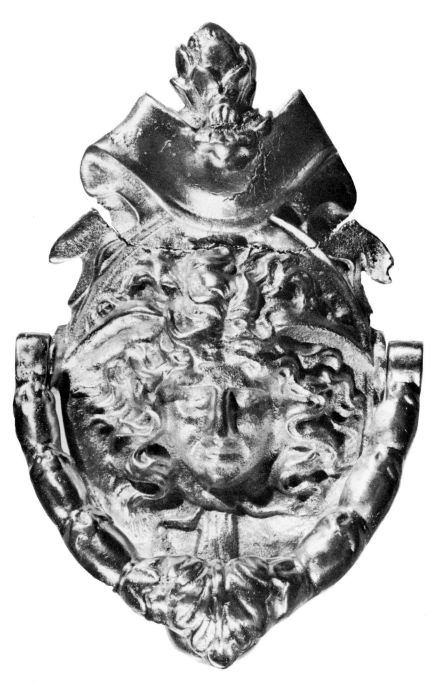

Among artifacts found at Williamsburg Printing Office site was a badly burned brass door knocker of the Neoclassical design popular in the eighteenth century.

powered by an urge to find out how a young man of Concord, who never before had been commissioned as a sculptor, had won the chance to design this memorial to the first American war heroes. In two years of snatching spare moments, I exhausted the shelves of near-by public libraries and searched through private papers. Finally I was able to piece together the story of how the sculptor who later was to create the Lincoln Memorial in Washington had won the Minute Man commission at the age of twenty-two by submitting a clay model in competition with established artists. French had used pictures of relatives who resembled Isaac Davis, the Acton captain killed at Old North Bridge, and had enlisted his father's farm overseer to pose while he shaped the statue's strong arms. These and many other details were published for the first time and I found myself with something of a local reputation as a researcher.

The beginnings of a sculpture cast from bronze must seem inconsequential. Yet beginnings are always more important than we are apt to recognize immediately. Beginnings, after all, form the basis of archaeology. My own beginnings, in the pursuit of all the facts about this symbol of independence, brought me into abrupt contact with the need to dig deeper—deeper and ever deeper.

Later, I took the same approach to a similar project. During the period when surgeons were introducing refrigeration as an anaesthetic, I was persuaded to search out the roots of the Vermont legend of human hibernation. One distinguished surgeon wrote me that a nineteenth-century account telling how Vermonters put aged persons to sleep in the snow was so "scientifically comparable with our laboratory experiences that real credence can be given the event which up to this time has been more or less legendary." I didn't have to dig in the earth, but I spent exhausting hours going through newspaper files and exploring attics before I finally tracked down the first published version of this startling story. It proved, indeed, to be legendary: A back-country yarn-spinner had embellished a tale of pure invention with ideas that happened to coincide with a twentieth-century theory of anaesthesia. Most people had regarded the legend with amusement, but only research going all the way back to the source could prove that the tale of human hibernation—the temporary disposal of those who couldn't earn their keep during the long winters—was not as plausible as the surgeon thought.

The inescapable prelude to all archaeological work is research. "Between archaeology and history," says Sir Leonard Woolley, discoverer of Ur, "there is no fenced frontier." The two are interlocked. The digger who first exhausts the written record becomes the successful archaeologist.

My own career of digging in the ground—rather than in the library—began, as it were, in the nineteenth century at Walden, slipped back two hundred years when I went to the Saugus Ironworks site, back six hundred more when we dug in search of a Viking encampment. Since then I have dug repeatedly in each of the centuries of European settlement in America.

2

"Go Thou My Incense Upward from This Hearth"

ACROSS THE BACK YARDS and under the old trees I might have walked to Walden Pond, following a vanished path made a hundred years before by a man whose strolls regularly had taken him across my own small piece of land. It was an excursion I had never made. I'd driven past that little lake in going from one window-cleaning job to another; I'd seen crowds of swimmers in the dusty days of summer, and ramshackle buildings hastily thrown up to attract hungry and thirsty visitors. But among the trees surrounding the pond, where Henry David Thoreau had lived a century ago, was buried a mystery about which I knew nothing.

Thoreau became something less of a mystery to me on Independence Day in 1945. I'd been invited, because of my recently expressed interest in Concord's past, to join those who had come

The Walden house was drawn by Thoreau's sister, Sophia, as
a frontispiece of the first edition, privately printed, of *Walden*.

hundreds of miles to celebrate the centennial anniversary of
Thoreau's first day of residence at Walden. Yet it was only a casual
invitation; I knew Thoreau simply as one of Concord's literary
heroes, and archaeology—so soon to become my abiding pre-
occupation—was just a word to me. I'd never dug anything—not
even a garden behind my house.

For a moment when I saw the sun emerge so brilliantly into a
cloudless sky on that Fourth of July, I put all thought of Walden
out of my mind. It was perfect summer weather—tennis weather.

"Go Thou My Incense Upward from This Hearth"

During the previous week while I was painting a house in Belmont, I'd been itching to get out onto a court, and as this holiday began I was tempted to forget the Thoreau centennial. I don't know now what caused me to repress the urge, but in retrospect it seems almost incredible that in the woods of Walden before that sunny day was over I had dedicated myself to a life of digging.

Yellow light sifted through the leaves at Walden in shafts and splotches. Strangers stood silently, or sat on stumps and patches of grass, listening to speeches about a young man who in 1845 had borrowed an ax from Bronson Alcott and felled young pine trees, cut mortises and tenons to raise a shelter remote from civilization. Later, as the commemorative exercises dissolved into conversations, I began to feel that the unavoidable challenge of the day was less in the philosophy of Thoreau than it was in the fact that no one among all these historians, teachers, and dedicated Thoreauvians knew exactly the site of the building which was so central a part of the writing of *Walden*.

Here in the woods the memorial cairn—made of stones brought from many parts of the country—was tangible enough. So was the bronze plaque which asserted that it marked the spot where Thoreau had built. Yet there had been, I discovered, a running debate, begun soon after Bronson Alcott had brought the first stones to the site in 1872. Some protested that the description of the terrain in *Walden* conflicted with the conformations surrounding the mounds of stones. Others seemed certain, even though it was known that Thoreau's one-room house had been moved to a Concord bean field soon after it was vacated, that some vestige must still exist—if only someone had the enterprise to find it. This scholarly quandary intrigued me as I stood by, listening to the talk. There were those who seemed to know Thoreau's Walden

Path along north shore of Walden Pond leading to Thoreau's cove, as it appeared in a late nineteenth-century photograph.

well and who believed that twenty-five or thirty years earlier the cairn had been much closer to the pond. Pointing to the relatively level ground at the site of the cairn, one man underscored his argument by recalling that in *Walden* Thoreau says: "My house was on the side of a hill—half a dozen rods from the pond." Even

Thoreau's cove as seen from the high ground known as Emerson's Cliff.

this seemed inconclusive, for there were others who thought an author was always entitled to poetic license and might have changed such a description to fit his mood.

"Maybe," the skeptic said. "But you must remember that Henry Thoreau was a surveyor—by eye alone almost as accurate as with a measuring tool. Even blindfolded, he couldn't have stretched that half-dozen rods from the shore to reach the spot where the cairn now sits."

When it became apparent that no one knew the length of a rod, there was a general embarrassment relieved only by another

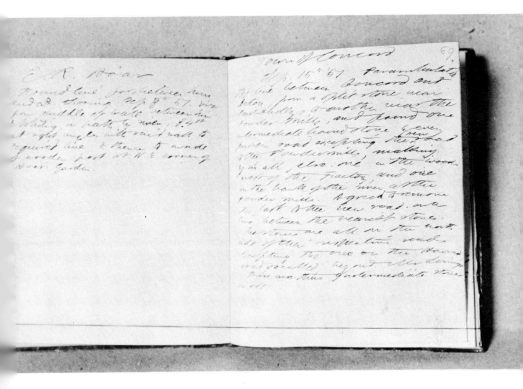

Thoreau filled pages of bound notebooks with the journals on which he based the much worked-over text of *Walden*.

quotation from Thoreau: "As I sit at my window this summer afternoon . . . a mink steals out of the marsh before my door and seizes a frog by the shore." The cairn was too far from the water for Thoreau to have seen an object the size of a frog, and, in addition, the view was obstructed by a knoll. This was enough to

"Go Thou My Incense Upward from This Hearth"

convince me that there was no certainty about the spot which had inspired the classic *Walden,* and I went home to mull over my first challenge in the science of digging.

To begin, I had to read *Walden* for the first time, hoping that the author himself might prove my most dependable guide. Not yet being able to visualize the structure, either in design or size, and confused by the customary mention of it as a hut, sometimes as a cabin, or even as a shack, I made an inventory, as I read the book, of the words Thoreau used to describe his home. More than eighty times, I found, he referred to it as a house; three times he called it a lodge, twice a dwelling, twice an apartment, and once a homestead. Hut appears only once. A visual impression seemed to me imperative, and I made note of further evidence in Thoreau's references to his plastering, his brick chimney, his fireplace, and a cellar hole "six feet square by seven feet deep" which he had dug "to a fine sand where potatoes would not freeze in any winter. The sides were left shelving, and not stoned. . . ." Reading this, I felt I was getting a reasonably accurate mental picture of the house; yet I could understand how its small size, coupled with its isolated location in what was then considered a forest wilderness, could have been responsible for the many misnomers applied to it. I found a further description in *Walden:* ". . . a tight shingled and plastered house, ten feet wide and fifteen long, eight-foot posts, with a garret and a closet, a large window on each side, two trap-doors, one door at the end, and a brick fireplace opposite. The exact cost . . . was $28.12½."

Not content with my purchase of a ninety-five-cent edition of the book, I also studied the marginal notes that Ellery Channing had made in the copy of *Walden* given him by his friend Thoreau. Many years after the house had been moved from the woods to the farm in Concord, Channing had observed: "The house stood in perfect condition so far as the frame and covering, to June 4,

'68, a period of twenty-three years, and would have lasted a century." Channing even corrected Thoreau's references to the location of the house at Walden. In an earlier note beside Thoreau's sentence, "I dug my cellar in the side of a hill," Channing wrote somewhat testily: "There is nothing like a hill here and never was. At present (Oct. '63), I tried with Mr. Green to find the cellar hole but could not fix it." He added later: ". . . but have since. It is in the pathway to the pond." These, it seemed to me, were clues to be interpreted before I started to dig, and I carefully compiled all the observations that seemed pertinent. Yet I could fit none of them into the landscape when I returned to Walden. It was almost by accident, while skirting the cairn with a companion, that I came upon three fragments of red brick embedded in the soil. Because Thoreau was said to have been the only person to have brought bricks into the woods, those clay pieces looked to me like gems.

But chips of bricks did not necessarily point to the house itself, and it occurred to me then that perhaps I had overlooked another important source: *Walden* was said to be based on journals Thoreau kept during his two years in the woods. I went again to the library. Again I was disappointed. The journals were extremely scanty and I discovered for the first time that *Walden* actually had been written about two years after Thoreau had left the pond; the notes had been blown up to book proportions with the aid of his memory and his imagination. Understanding this, I was moved to wonder how much I might be able to depend on any of the book's descriptions. Of all my clues now, those brick fragments were the only leads that seemed to warrant immediate pursuit. I requested official permission from the Superintendent of the Walden Pond State Reservation to start an excavation in the vicinity of the cairn.

To help me locate solid objects I conceived a new tool—I had a blacksmith make a four-foot steel rod, one-half inch thick, with a handle at one end and a sharp point at the other. I bought a pocket compass, a ninety-eight-cent GI trench shovel, and several pairs of canvas gloves. With these, I became an archaeologist; anyway, I started to dig. In the area where I had picked up the three fragments, I hoped my new tools would be led to something bigger. I removed the turf in cautious spadefuls, piling it near by ready for replacement. I lifted out the under soil, sifting it with my fingers. Almost immediately I was rewarded. Within a space eight feet long, three feet wide at its greatest width, and from two to seven inches beneath the surface of the ground, I scraped out one hundred pieces of brick ranging from three quarters of an inch to a third of a brick in size. I felt sure that in some way at last I had come across Thoreau's trail.

That afternoon I drove to Cambridge to have a brick expert examine the fragments. He found them to be old water-struck handmade bricks—a type that had been shaped in water-lubricated molds instead of in the sand molds now commonly in use. As elation began to mount within me, I thought of a passage in *Walden*: "When I came to build my chimney," Thoreau had written, "I studied masonry. My bricks being second-hand ones required to be cleaned with a trowel. . . . The mortar on them was fifty years old, and was said to be still growing harder. . . ."

The bricks I had found were old and handmade, but how old was old? "Could they be a century and a half old?" I asked.

"Easily."

I tasted victory as I heard that word.

But the joy ebbed away when I went back to digging, for I found nothing more at my site—there was no sign of the mortar that Thoreau told of chipping off the bricks. Still, something made me sure that these pieces were from the "one thousand old brick" which Thoreau had purchased for four dollars in order to build his fireplace. I began to develop a theory: perhaps in carrying the bricks from his unloading pile to the site of his chimney, Thoreau had stumbled; picking up only the whole bricks, he might have left the useless pieces where they had fallen, for erosion and slope-wash to shield and keep for me.

On Sunday, October 21, I got up early and headed for the woods, determined to locate the place where Thoreau had piled the bricks during the course of building his fireplace. One spot, investigated in an earlier (and inaccurate) effort to identify the site of the house itself, drew me for reasons I couldn't rationalize. Here, on a hill side fifty-odd feet northwest of the cairn, was what appeared to be an excavation just the right size to accommodate the dimensions of Thoreau's structure, but its position was so concealed and so isolated (it had no such view of the pond as described in *Walden*) that I had eliminated it as the goal of my principal search. Nevertheless, it beckoned me now.

I cut into the soil with my shovel and immediately turned up brick particles. All that day and through the morning of the following Sunday I dug persistently, grappling with the network of roots which seemed almost humanly zealous in guarding my quarry. Before I was finished—from an area twelve feet square and two to seven inches deep—I had removed several thousand pieces of brick, most of them rather small. And I found no sign of mortar. There seemed little doubt now that this was where the load of "one thousand old brick" had been piled or dumped when first brought to the pond.

I visualized a line starting at this point and crossing the spot where I'd come across the first three fragments, reasoning that Thoreau must have walked in this direction, perhaps stumbling, as he carried his bricks to build his fireplace. Thrusting my probe rod into the ground at intervals on the following Sunday, I struck a solid object embedded about a foot in the earth, and almost directly beneath the stump of a white pine tree. Shoveling then,

"Go Thou My Incense Upward from This Hearth"

I turned over the earth and found white plaster. It was a moment of real excitement, for in spite of the stump, I was sure that at last I'd hit pay dirt. Large pieces of brick encrusted with mortar followed, and then I turned up several badly rusted, square-cut nails. Within fifteen minutes I had one ten-quart pail filled with pieces of plaster, and another with brick. Some of the pieces were smoke-blackened.

Absorbed in the certainty that at my feet were remnants of Thoreau's chimney, I dug on with no awareness of anything outside myself until I heard a youthful voice ask: "What are you digging for?"

On the rim of my excavation stood two soldiers, sergeant's stripes on their sleeves, their blouses distinguished by the Army Air Force insignia, campaign ribbons, and the Presidential citation. The one thought uppermost in my mind as I looked up was that it was too soon to share what I was sure I had discovered. I tried to parry the all-too-direct questions about Thoreau and Walden. But in a moment it became apparent that these visitors had felt more than idle curiosity when they had stumbled upon me.

"Sorry to be bothering you," one of the boys said, "but I'm a distant relative of Henry David Thoreau." As I watched his face, I had the feeling that he was telling me the truth. "I'm on my way home to California from the E.T.O.," he went on. "I've never been here before and may never have a chance again, so I'm anxious to learn as much as I can of Walden."

Now it was I who was curious. "Mind my asking your name?"

"Henry David Thoreau, Jr.," he said.

On top of my exhilaration over the evidence under the stump, this seemed too much for one day, yet there was more to come. Beyond the soldiers I saw a member of the Thoreau Society who lived in Concord approaching us. At this point in my excavation

I would have been happier with no onlookers at all, for I wanted to erase every lurking doubt before I was called upon to discuss the find. Perhaps the appearance of Sergeant Thoreau was a good omen, I thought, but I wasn't sure that I could handle any other distractions. Still, I couldn't avoid introducing the lean, young relative of Walden's first settler.

Yankee humor sparkled in the eyes of my Concord friend. "How do you do, Mr. Thoreau," he said; then, smiling wryly, he turned to the other soldier. "And who is this? Ralph Waldo Emerson?"

To the boys it didn't seem funny. Sergeant Thoreau pulled out his dog tags to prove his identity.

The next Sunday, November 4, we had an unseasonable snowstorm. From the windows of my own house I saw the ground covered and for a moment felt disheartened. Winter seemed about to put an end to my digging. But there was at least one thing I could accomplish above ground. I called John Lambert, a state forestry expert who lived in Concord, and persuaded him to help determine the age of the tree stump that was straddling my mine of bricks and mortar.

The Walden woods were covered with their burden of white as we slogged through the brush that afternoon. Now I was unable to walk among those trees without being reminded of Walden as it had been seen by Thoreau: "The snow lying deep on the earth dotted with young pines, and the very slope of the hill on which my house is placed seemed to say, Forward!" It was a line which that day I felt had been written for me. Thoreau's young pines had grown up and seeded others, and under the stump of one of them was the evidence by which I hoped to establish beyond any doubt the exact location of the house that had become an American literary landmark.

Pausing with Jack Lambert, I looked down at the hole I had dug. "Standing on the snow-covered plain," Thoreau had written,

"Go Thou My Incense Upward from This Hearth"

"as if in a pasture amid the hills, I cut my way first through a foot of snow, and then a foot of ice, and open a window under my feet. . . ." With John's help in dendrochronology, the study of tree rings to determine age, I hoped to open a figurative window that would show how long ago the bricks and mortar had been buried. When finally he turned from his meticulous count of the rings in the stump, Lambert said: "Eighty-three years—a year one way or the other. It was felled by the 1938 hurricane, so it began its growth about 1855."

It was evident that the white pine could not have taken root in this spot until roughly eight years after Thoreau's house had been moved to the bean field; for ninety years its roots had been protecting the two hundred and seventy-six pounds of bricks, plaster, and nails I'd exposed. But to allay any possible doubt, I rechecked the story of another squatter who had built a cabin on the shores of Walden Pond. He was Edmund Stuart Hotham, a New York theological student who had emulated Thoreau by erecting his own shelter and living in it from November 1869 to May 1870. The white pine stump proved that the relics shielded by its roots were unrelated to any building Hotham might have done—for the tree had been seeded and had taken possession of this soil fourteen years before Hotham came to the woods. I consulted one more authority. In the notes of Ellery Channing I found the statement: "Hotham's cabin was by the pond on the bank, in front of Henry's"; no house located near the stump could be described as being "on the bank."

During that week, I continued to dig in the hard earth at a point about three feet north of the stump, and found pieces of uneven, hand-poured bluish window glass, with putty still clinging to the edge of one fragment; I uncovered fragments of an old tumbler, as well as other glass that seemed to have been part of a vase or a jar. Yet, though more handmade nails turned up when I sifted the soil,

Roland Robbins and John Lambert saw a section from the white-pine stump to determine its age.

I seemed to be no closer to uncovering the foundation of the chimney Thoreau's water-struck bricks had formed.

One evening at the Concord Library I met a member of the Thoreau Society and told him my doubts about ever locating the foundation. "I've been all over the hillside with probing rods and shovels," I said ruefully. "I've blistered my hands so that I sometimes wish I'd never have to touch a shovel again. There are plenty of small clues like nails and bricks, but not a thing to lead me to the chimney base." The Thoreauvian's effort to cheer me didn't help much; the vanished fireplace site just didn't make sense. "We know the chimney had a foundation," I said, "and foundations aren't salvaged when buildings are moved."

Even the weather was mournful. Armistice Day came on Sunday. It was a raw day, streaming with rain. The woods oozed with water; every leaf held a puddle, every twig drowsed in a mire, the

"Go Thou My Incense Upward from This Hearth"

wintry soil sucked audibly at my boots. But because the frost could come suddenly to stake its own claim at my dig, I decided to make one more effort to find the hearth. I was convinced that, if it still existed, it had to be in the area which had produced the artifacts. So I dug deeper at the spot in which I had dug before. When I found more nails twelve inches below the natural surface, I attributed their depth to erosion; it seemed unreasonable that nails should sink so far under their own weight. Almost futilely I thrust my probe rod into this soil, and at a depth of more than two feet I struck something solid. Although I was pessimistic enough to think that nothing helpful to me could be so far down, I scraped the damp earth away and exposed a large, fairly flat boulder. When I pushed my rod at several points near this stone, the steel rang again as it clashed with whatever lay buried. I plunged the rod in once more and heard the ring of metal against hard rock. Only then did it occur to me that erosion, or man, or both, might have covered Henry Thoreau's chimney base with so thick a coating of earth. Taking up the trench shovel, I quickly stripped away that natural camouflage to uncover two boulders joined together with lime mortar. Further digging revealed what proved to be the southwest corner of the much debated, long-sought chimney foundation. I looked up, this time eager to find someone with whom I could share my excitement. But I could see no one, for the end of the winter day had come, and the pines of Walden shut out the rest of the world.

That evening I called Aaron Bagg, who at the centennial exercises had urged me to attempt the Walden dig, and asked him to join me the next morning in exposing the entire foundation. Dawn brought the same foul weather, and we stooped and scraped in the freezing, ceaseless drizzle, working with a caution that kept us at

Sinking a probe rod under white-pine stump led to discovery of the Walden house site.

A brick and pieces of mortar found at the site of Thoreau's chimney.

the task longer than we had anticipated. The dark trees closed in on us just as we finished. The rain caused the stones to glisten in the gloom. It was not a structure made of boulders alone, for the northeast corner was formed of broken brick that hadn't been suitable for the chimney. Brick also was used for wedging purposes, to fill small crevices. Mortar had been used only in key positions, to bind the corners of the foundation, and to hold brick and boulder together. The structure measured five feet in both directions, an almost perfect square. Only the stones of the hearth were missing, and this fact corroborated Ellery Channing's notation that the hearth had been removed by the man who hauled the house to the bean field. That day provided another coincidence. In 1845 Thoreau had written in his journal: "Left house on account of plastering, Wednesday, November 12th, at night. . . ." Exactly one hundred years after the Walden house was finished (for its construction was not complete until it was plastered) its chimney foundation was exposed once more to the light of day.

During the next week, members of the Thoreau Society came to see for themselves; the site was photographed, and I recorded my compass readings of the position. Then, placing one of my painter's drop cloths over the foundation, I covered it carefully with turf, packing it down and leveling it so that little evidence of this excavation should remain. I had to wait until the next year to find the storage cellar hole that Thoreau had dug beneath the house.

As Thoreau had written: "The oaks, hickories, maples, and other trees, just putting out amidst the pine woods around the pond, imparted a brightness like sunshine to the landscape, especially in cloudy days, as if the sun were breaking through mists and shining faintly on the hillsides here and there."

On just such a day I renewed my investigations on the periphery of the area where I had covered the foundation stones. More century-old nails came to light, and soon I unearthed the northwest foundation stone of the house. When Memorial Day morning came, I picked wild flowers and ferns from the site and took them to Sleepy Hollow Cemetery in Concord to place on Thoreau's grave. That afternoon I found a scarified piece of lead—a sinker Thoreau might have used for fishing. On the Fourth of July the year in which I had been involved with Henry Thoreau came to an end. I spent the morning digging behind the chimney base, and that day, one hundred and one years after Thoreau had moved in, I located the southeast corner foundation of his woodshed. It was buried a foot and a half in the soil and was constructed of bricks and stones.

On Tuesday morning, August 13, accompanied by Raymond Emerson of Concord, a grandson of Thoreau's mentor, I visited the Middlesex County Commissioners to obtain permission to remove a section of the cairn covering what I now was convinced was the site of the cellar hole. Fixed in my mind was the description from

"Go Thou My Incense Upward from This Hearth"

Walden: "I dug my cellar in the side of a hill sloping to the south, where a woodchuck had formerly dug his burrow, down through sumach and blackberry roots, and the lowest stain of vegetation, six feet square by seven deep, to a fine sand where potatoes would not freeze in the winter. The sides were left shelving, and not stoned; but the sun having never shone on them, the sand still keeps its place. It was but two hours work. I took particular pleasure in this breaking of ground, for in almost all latitudes men dig into the earth for an equable temperature. Under the most splendid house in the city is still to be found the cellar where they store their roots as of old, and long after the superstructure has disappeared posterity remarks its dent in the earth. The house is still but a sort of porch at the entrance of a burrow."

Now, however, no depression remained to lead us to the Walden cellar. The surface soil of the filled-in hole was a layer of humus that had accumulated during the twenty-five-year period between the moving of the house in 1847 and the construction of the stone cairn in 1872. Two feet beneath the humus, with the help of my friend Anton Kovar, I found bent and rusted square nails, pieces of plaster, pottery, and glass, and wood ashes. Five feet beneath the humus the sandy soil was mixed with rich soil. Because we found no relics deeper than thirty inches, it became apparent that a load of fill had been carted in and dumped in the cellar after the house was transplanted. The top fill had come from around the house site, accounting for the artifacts found near the surface.

We were persuaded to close up this excavation, but before we did so Walter Harding, secretary of the Thoreau Society, wrote a statement which we sealed in a bottle and buried where Thoreau had kept his "firkin of potatoes, about two quarts of peas with the weevil in them, and on my shelf a little rice, a jug of molasses, and of rye and Indian meal a peck each."

The statement says: "The undersigned have witnessed the ex-

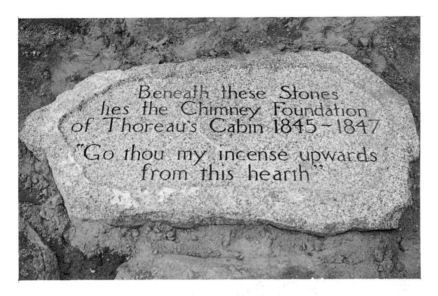

A slab of granite brought from the farm on which Thoreau was born marks the exact site of the chimney foundation.

cavation of the cellar hole of Henry David Thoreau's Walden cabin on Labor Day, September 2, 1946, by Roland Wells Robbins who discovered the site of the chimney foundation on November 11, 1945." It was signed by nine visitors who had gathered that day. Later the ground plan of the house was marked with granite posts and over the fireplace foundation was placed a flat stone we selected from the farm on which Thoreau had been born. Engraved in this New England rock is the line from *Walden*: "Go thou my incense upward from this hearth."

No longer was it true that Henry David Thoreau "gave notice to the various wild inhabitants of Walden vale by a smoky streamer from my chimney." But after one hundred years, for all pilgrims to Walden Pond, the house's site and the fireplace from which that smoky streamer rose were fixed beyond dispute.

One of the early maps of Saugus shows the ironworks straddling
the Saugus River, surrounded by hills and woods.

3

The Water Wheel under Central Street

Ten miles north of Boston is the old town of Saugus. A decade ago its citizens knew little of what riches lay buried beneath them. True, a weathered "iron master's house" still stood on the outskirts of town and under this colonial roof a local historical group met periodically to discuss Saugus's beginning years as the home of a thriving ironworks. Brush and poison ivy covered the low ground across from the three-hundred-year-old house on Central Street, and old-timers sometimes dreamed of erecting a replica of a colonial factory as a reminder of the town's past glory. But when I was asked to take part in what one called "an antique treasure hunt," there seemed little faith that the earth would yield anything more than the stones which had comprised the foundation of a blast furnace.

Today the Saugus visitor finds Central Street blocked off; as if he had abruptly left the twentieth century, he sees below him the ancient ironworks as it appeared in the middle of the seventeenth century. It is a restoration which Richard Howland, President of the National Trust for Historic Preservation, called "the most accurate in America," a re-creation of colonial life made possible by the finds my tools uncovered during almost five years of digging. It stands as concrete proof of the vast amount of American history which lies under our feet, waiting only for us to dig it out.

I first came into contact with this particular bit of buried history in September 1948 when a man who had heard of my discovery at Walden invited me to hunt treasure at Saugus. I sat in the museum-like ironmaster's house with J. Sanger Attwill, president of the Saugus group known as the First Ironworks Association. "We're interested," Mr. Attwill said, "in locating the site of the ancient ironworks which was producing both cast and wrought iron more than three centuries ago."

It was the sudden thought of men at work three hundred years before my own time which captured my imagination. When I had been immersed in Thoreau and digging in the woods at Walden, the past of a century ago had seemed an eternity away. I rarely thought of the history of the United States as pre-dating the Revolutionary War, yet here I was, a rank amateur—happily with some free time while I waited for the storm-window season—being asked to dig for remnants of a thriving industry, created only a few years after the first Pilgrim had set foot on Massachusetts soil.

Mr. Attwill stood at the window and pointed across Central Street at the low, swampy area. "Logic tends to support the local legend that this is the site," he said. "But we have no plans, sketches, or real information."

The challenge appealed to me. As I walked across the street with Sanger Attwill, I noticed the terrain; it formed a kind of natural amphitheater past which the Saugus River flowed to the

Atlantic. Here certainly was enough water power for a colonial industry. If you blocked off from view the contemporary buildings on the adjacent land, you could fairly imagine the water wheel that must have disintegrated long ago: yet in the boggy ground there must still be stones that had been used to build a furnace. Who knew what other clues might still be buried? The men who had worked and lived at this site had brought to America the basic skills which were later perfected in the great foundries of Youngstown and Bethlehem. Perhaps under this earth these men had left behind a tool or an example of the articles they had manufactured here. If this was indeed the site of the first iron-manufacturing plant built in the American colonies, it seemed to me to deserve investigation at least as thorough as the digging done by Egyptologists. And certainly it offered an opportunity I did not want to miss.

Pushing my way through the tangled vegetation that afternoon I found several spots at which slag—the scum thrown off from molten metal—was visible above the surface. Using the technique that had aided me at Walden, I went over the ground with my probe rod, plunging it in at intervals in the hope of finding something that might be related to the blast furnace. I cleared away some of the brush and in digging turned up a single nail that appeared to be very old, fragments of bricks and stones which looked as if they might have been subjected to intense heat, a one-inch piece of a clay pipe, and some charcoal. None of this was in any way conclusive of anything, but it seemed to me encouraging.

I soon found that the earth which bordered the river had been stoned up at one time in an apparent effort to retain an abundance of scoria; in one spot my test showed a deposit of this slaggy refuse to a depth of at least three feet. The deposits took the general shape of a crescent leading from the river toward the embankment

The Water Wheel under Central Street

Early ironworks, as shown in Diderot's encyclopedia of arts and methods, was similar in many ways to the establishment beside the Saugus River.

dropping away from Central Street, and it seemed logical to me that the furnace must have been at the end of the crescent farthest from the river. I started digging in this area on my third day at Saugus.

At depths of one foot and fifteen inches I turned up small pieces of chinaware. Putting them aside, I knew I would have to have an expert determine whether or not they belonged to the seventeenth century. At two feet six inches my shovel uncovered a bed of baked clay which had turned red in color, and next to it pieces of quarried sandstone and small pieces of charcoal. The bed of clay varied from six to nine inches in thickness, and under it, on the exposure facing the river, I found a layer of medium-sized stones.

Drawing from Diderot's encyclopedia shows methods of pouring molten iron into sand forms—manual operations identical with those carried on at Saugus.

On the other side of the clay bed, facing Central Street, was a layer of very white fine sand. I pushed my rod down through the sand to a depth of five and a half feet and found no suggestion of a foundation. Then I began digging a trench toward the river, following the stone base beneath the bed of clay. At the point where stones and sand met I found charcoal embedded almost three feet deep.

The next day I was visited by Quincy Bent, a retired vice-president of Bethlehem Steel Company and a member of the First Iron-works Association, and he seemed impressed. He lined up other

The Water Wheel under Central Street

affluent Association members, who agreed that I should continue digging for a month and that I should be given enough money to provide labor and equipment and a salary for myself.

That week I signed on my first crew—three talented diggers from the Saugus Water Department—to work evenings, Saturdays, and Sundays. I bought shovels, pickaxes, stiff brooms, and brushes, and explained to my men that archaeological digging required even greater caution than they were accustomed to use in their excavation of the city's plumbing system. They caught on immediately and learned to handle the tools as temperately as a barber uses a straight-edge razor.

Six days after I had been given the go-ahead, one of the men spotted a white clay pipe as we were uncovering the stone base. He held it out to me. Half of its bowl was missing, but on the front I could make out an insignia with the initials T.D.; also engraved on it were a scroll and a simple border. Though it turned out to be

At Saugus, as in this Diderot illustration, hot iron was shaped on sand beds into long bars for convenient handling.

one of the commonest types of pipes smoked during the nineteenth century, my spirits rose at the sight of it. We began to find metal bars among the stones, and on the first Sunday in October one of the workmen turned up a second clay pipe, this one with a Grecian scroll around the top of the bowl. Two days later we located two large pieces of cast iron on the outer edge of the charcoal bed; one of these weighed more than a hundred pounds. Then we found pig iron pieces that had solidified in the casting-sands in the shape of triangular bars. On October 9 we found parts of kettle castings. These were our first discoveries of utensils that had been manufactured at Saugus.

As the digging went on we often had more visitors than workmen. Kids scrambled down the embankment on their way home from school, and more than once I was able to make real use of them. They were interested enough to accept small chores with enthusiasm. One of them, who shared the early discoveries with

The eighteenth-century encyclopedia shows the operation of a giant hammer similar to the one unearthed at Saugus.

Interlocked beams formed base for two great bellows which fanned the furnace constructed of the stones shown in background.

us, became a guide for the Restoration that eventually followed our excavations. He stood by, watching, the day I scraped away the earth from two great wooden beams that ran in a V-shape toward the center of the stone foundation. These timbers suddenly seemed to give shape to what had seemed a formless pile of boulders, and I was now convinced that the stones had been the furnace.

"What's the wood doing there?" the boy asked.

I told him to climb down into the pit. "You know what a bellows looks like, Clyde? See how these beams follow the same general shape? Just imagine them as a cradle holding giant bellows."

He seemed confused.

"Look, Clyde," I said, pointing to the tapering pipe embedded in the earth at the end of the beams. "Remember how perplexed I was about that pipe when we uncovered it the other day? These timbers you can see leading to that pipe supported the pair of leather bellows that supplied air to keep the furnace going. That's why it's called a blast furnace."

Clyde began to get the picture. "Because of the bellows?"

"Right. The bellows blasted the air through that funnel-like nozzle directly onto the hearth, keeping the fires going twenty-four hours a day. Without that blast they couldn't have created a fire hot enough to smelt the ore."

"All that charcoal you've been finding is left over from those fires," Clyde said enthusiastically.

He was right again. At the furnace's center we had unearthed an eight-foot-square crucible pit from which a charcoal bed wedged out in an easterly direction. Though the foundation proved to be about twenty-five feet square when we excavated its perimeter, there had been an opening large enough to house the bellows on one side, and at right angles on another side an opening for the beds of sand in which pig iron and items such as kettles and skillets were cast. Along the west side we exposed more beams that defined the shape of the raceway, the channel through which water flowed from the water wheel.

By this time I felt certain that the wheel that had powered the furnace bellows must have been situated northwest of the foundation, but this meant that the site lay buried under Central Street. No thought could have been more frustrating, for I couldn't then imagine that the town would let me dig under its blacktop—and, indeed, I had no invitation as yet to come back to excavate under any circumstances.

The Water Wheel under Central Street

Nevertheless I felt compelled to know as much as possible about this enterprise that, only a quarter-century after the landing at Plymouth, had helped to supply the colonists with pots to hang over their kitchen fires and with hardware to build many of the first American homes. Though I returned to my storm-window obligations, I was never far from Saugus in spirit, for I spent a good deal of that winter in libraries chasing down elusive bits about the organization and construction of seventeenth-century industries.

Saugus, three hundred years ago, was known as Hammersmith. To this river site, with its natural amphitheater, the colonial corporation known as "the Company of Undertakers for the Iron Works in New England" had come in 1646. John Winthrop, Jr., son of the governor of Massachusetts Bay Colony, and himself later governor of Connecticut, had been the enterprising promoter who had raised the money to get the company started. Records indicated he had also had an active role in the Braintree ironworks in what is now part of near-by West Quincy. Yet, though the magic of the Winthrop name is still linked with Saugus, it was a man named Richard Leader who proved to have been the engineering genius behind the now buried ironworks. It was Leader, in the company of friendly Indians, who surveyed the Boston region and discovered the Saugus River swamps, which contained "bog iron of good quality." It was he who saw in the high ground that framed the swamps the ideal answer to the problem of charging the furnace; at this site boats could sail in at high tide and be loaded directly from the works. Although such facts as these came to light, particularly after E. N. Hartley, the historian from M.I.T., joined the investigations, there were no descriptions of the structures that housed the Hammersmith operation nor any exact knowledge of the range of its activity. In that earth in which I'd found the ruins of a blast furnace were answers historians might

Jenkes mo:
nopolye

[handwritten manuscript text - early modern court record]

Jenkes mo-
nopolye

At a generall Courte at Boston
the 6th of the 3th m° 1646

The Co't consid'inge y° necessity of raising such manifactures of engins of mils to go
by water for speedy dispatch of much worke wth few hands, & being sufficiently informed
of y° ability of y° petition' to pforme such workes grant his petition (y° no oth° pson
shall set up, or use any such new invention, or trade for fourteen yeares wthout y° licence
of him y° said Joseph Jenkes) so farr as concernes any such new invention, & so as it shalbe
alwayes in y° pow' of this Co'te to restrain y° exportation of such manifactures & y° prizes
of them to moderation if occasion so require.

Joseph Jenk's "monopoly" to make engines for mills was the
first patent issued in America, dated March 6, 1646.

never find in their search of files and records. I became convinced
that by extending my trenches from the furnace site I would find
some of these answers. But as winter wore on I had only the hope
that new funds would be made available through the American
Iron and Steel Institute.

I pursued other clues as I waited. According to local legend,
Joseph Jenks had master-minded the iron works. Through research
and correspondence with his descendants I found this to be un-
true, but I did find him to be a fascinating figure. He was a black-
smith who, in 1646, took out the first machine patent in America:
for "engines of mills to go by water"; and Jenks also had a patent
for an improvement on the scythe. The legend said that he had
made the dies for the pine-tree shilling, which was the only legal
Massachusetts coinage between 1652 and 1684, and that he built
the first fire engine in the colonies. He was in fact a concessionaire

The Water Wheel under Central Street

47

of the ironworks. His small factory adjoined the furnace and refinery-forge from which he got the iron he fashioned into marketable items. The whole operation could therefore fairly be regarded as a forerunner of modern assembly-line production, and Jenks's activity here seemed to promise archaeological discoveries which would make the site of lasting importance.

Already our digging indicated that the Hammersmith plant was conceived as a unit and developed over a number of years as a complete and integrated ironworks. Deeds show that by January 1648, Richard Leader had come to an agreement with Jenks whereby the latter was to erect a "mill or hamer for the making of sithes or any other Iron ware by water at the taile of the furnace & to have the full benefit of the furnace water when the furnace goes." Jenks was to get from Leader "barr iron & cast iron for gudgins, shafts and hoopes." There was tempting evidence in these few lines that before Hammersmith had crumbled into ruins a good deal of Yankee enterprise had been demonstrated on these slopes beside the Saugus River.

That swampy acreage continued to lure me as I went about my winter business; yet, though I visited it repeatedly during the cold weather, it was not until the evening of March 28, 1949, that I got the telephone call for which I'd been waiting. It was Sanger Attwill; he had just talked to Quincy Bent. "Mr. Bent says the steel industry is behind us," Sanger said. "He wants you to get a crew and get started immediately."

The next day I sat in the ironmaster's house with Charles Rufus Harte and Miss Louise Hawkes, both active in the First Ironworks Association, discussing my plans for further excavation. And on Saturday, April 2, I began the work that was to last until the summer of 1953. Ed Higgins, Jim McCadden, and Tony Flammia, the same crew I'd had in the fall, signed on again, and we began digging at the corner of the furnace nearest Central Street, in search of the tailrace, the channel into which the wheel spilled its water.

We began finding artifacts that first afternoon and my three helpers were as eagle-eyed as I in spotting them. Part of a bar of iron was uncovered in the crucible pit, and near the tailrace area I found chunks of sandstone which clearly had been shattered by heat and which I deduced had been part of the crucible lining. For further study, I put these in the attic of the ironmaster's house, together with the tailrace timbers, square nails, a piece of rolled metal, a circular casting, and a clay saucer.

Digging beside the furnace wall to a depth of ten feet below the top of the remains, we found the floor of the tailrace, and in the soil which now filled this water channel were many relics, including more pig iron and pieces of iron kettles. But excavating the tailrace was far from easy because of the roots of a giant elm growing above it. It took a week after the tree was felled to dig out its roots. In the muddy, sloppy soils, with a pump operating to drain off the water that came from underground springs, we exposed the timbers that had lined the narrow raceway—fortuitously preserved by the springs. We also found pieces of unworked bog ore, charcoal, and slag.

With the course of the tailrace now definitely identified, most of the doubters seemed to agree that the furnace waterwheel must have turned in the area where Central Street now was. But to establish this beyond question meant tearing up the street and digging into the twelve-foot wall which supported it. And this in turn meant that a new route for Central Street traffic would have to be constructed and that at least one family would have to be evicted. Through a series of conferences we were able to persuade the sympathetic local officials; but it was not until September of 1950 that the project finally was approved in town meeting, and it was December before we were able to cut into the pavement. Still,

The Water Wheel under Central Street

the intervening months were not spent in idle waiting. I hired more diggers and started a systematic paring away of the top soils in an effort to get to the natural contours which had existed when Richard Leader had brought his workers to the site. Fanning out to the river we found buried in the mud some of the stones and timbers which had been used to construct the original riveryard. At the furnace I had already had the men shave the area down twenty-eight to thirty-two inches and we had found the casting-beds for both pig iron and household ware; they were hollowed out of a slope, lined with fine sand, and still contained fragments of the clay molds used by the colonists. In this area we uncovered the sprues and gates through which the molten iron had been poured to reach the molds.

All this time I was learning more about the iron business than I had ever dreamed of. Very little of what we were finding was easily recognizable, and as a result I spent a good deal of time tracking down every possible clue. Men in the steel industry who came to inspect the digging provided essential information, and I spent a day at an iron foundry studying modern methods and equipment to help me interpret the artifacts we were turning up. Neal Hartley and I drove to West Quincy to examine a site at which, it proved later, the forerunner of the Hammersmith Works had operated for several years. A test pit I sank at West Quincy revealed burned sandstone of the same nature as that at Saugus, and this helped to establish that the two operations were of the same era. Every fragment of information, no matter how insignificant it seemed, was valuable to me.

This was not like the dig in the Walden woods—for there I'd had Thoreau's description of his single building and my only problem was to locate its site. Here at Saugus, we didn't know what kind of structures had once stood nor how many specific activities had taken place in them. We were piecing together a buried and crumbled jigsaw puzzle, the size and design of which was a mystery.

One muggy August afternoon, for instance, I began to dig cautiously within a giant ring of rough metal which we had exposed. In the center, I found an almost perfect circle, forty-one inches in diameter, of strikingly black, rich soil—like an earthen bull's-eye. I sank my probe rod into it and felt the thump as it struck wood.

"What is it?" asked one of the men. "A tree that rotted out underground?"

"Must be more than that. Why would that metal shell be around a growing tree of this size?"

I dug down more than six feet and found that the ironmakers had cut a section from a giant oak, dug a hole into the ground, mounted the section on interlocked beams of oak, and used it as the base for their anvil. This device had been packed with a mixture of clay and slag, stabilizing it as if it were laid in cement. Half of it had been preserved by the water table; the other half had disintegrated into friable soil. And on closer examination the metal shell proved to be formed of the accumulation of impurities hammered out of molten iron. Seepage had caused these impurities to rust and eventually to solidify in the shape of a ring.

Three weeks later, while we were working in the rain, Mike Bucchiere grunted when his pick gave a sharp, muffled ping as it bit into the earth.

"Got a bite, Mike?"

"It's a big 'un," he said.

I dropped to my knees and began to scrape away the earth. At six inches below the surface the corner of a solid iron object came to light. Digging around it, I uncovered a giant hammer head—about three feet from nose to base. After several workmen pulled it out, we had it weighed. It tipped the scales at five hundred and five pounds; later it was determined that those extra five pounds

The Water Wheel under Central Street

Six men worked hard to remove the five-hundred-pound hammer found at the forge site.

could be accounted for by the encrustation of gravel and soil.

These finds were the first steps toward identifying the refinery forge, a barn-like frame structure that included three hearths and four water wheels. On one side of this forge building, large bellows fanned a chafery—the hearth at which the malleable iron was reheated and drawn out into finished bars. On the other side was the finery, the hearth that melted down pig iron, removed the carbon, and provided the heat to bring it to a semi-finished state. Both these hearths were worked in conjunction with the big hammer. The giant cast-iron head had studded a heavy oak helve mounted between wooden legs and raised by cams on a water-wheel shaft. In trip-hammer operation the five-hundred-pound head was raised and lowered by water power, falling on an anvil set on the oak block I had found half decayed. I felt that I could almost see the red-hot bloom of cooked iron being squeezed into shape under the hammer, the sprays of liquid fire sizzling about the forge as the impurities were beaten out.

Already our finds were shaping the picture of what life beside the Saugus River had been like in the 1640's. The blast furnace, which I'd discovered first, had been built on the westerly slope of the natural amphitheater, after the ground had been cut away and leveled to accommodate it. About twenty-one feet high, with slightly sloping outer walls of fieldstone, its top was reached by a wooden bridge over which the iron workers brought the materials that charged the furnace. About three tons of bog ore and 265 bushels of charcoal were required to make a ton of crude iron.

In the furnace's sandstone-lined crucible a fluxing agent was dumped to help separate iron from the natural impurities in the ore as it was smelted; the molten metal, being heavier, collected at the bottom and was run off through sand trenches into the casting-beds we had excavated. Here it was shaped into the triangular pigs. It also was ladled into clay molds for hollow ware. Back at the crucible was the underground drainage system I had found, which was designed to safeguard the liquid iron from any chance contact with moisture, a hazard caused by natural seepage.

The site of the furnace water wheel lay buried under Central Street until the winter of 1950-1. For six weeks, in weather that ranged from eight-inch snowfalls to all-day rains, from zero to 66 degrees in temperature, through three feet of frost, we hacked away at Central Street, using mechanical equipment to dispose of

The Water Wheel under Central Street

53

tons of fill. My test-trenching had revealed an earlier road-bed only nine inches beneath the blacktop, and under this a bed of rich soil that sloped from twenty-five inches under the street to thirty-seven inches. This was an even earlier surface. At this level a depression, sunk in the natural sand and now filled with slag, gravel, and more charcoal, proved to be the water course to the furnace water wheel. As we dug deeper into this with our shovels and grub-hoes we found more and more charcoal, many nails of the colonial period, and other clear evidence that the site of the water course had been filled in deliberately, probably late in the seventeenth century.

As these artifacts piled up in the temporary museum building I now had, I had become concerned about proper treatment and had been trying various methods of preservation. As the result of requests for advice, I was visited one cold February morning by Professor Herbert Uhlig of M.I.T. He was amazed at the amount of iron we were finding.

"Three hundred years is a lot longer than most metals last underground," he said, picking up an ancient iron weight I'd found. "Have you had any of these pieces analyzed?"

I got out the report from Bethlehem Steel which indicated that nickel was part of the Hammersmith formula.

"Nickel would have tended to preserve the iron," Uhlig said. "And what about the soil? Any evidence of alkali?"

"At one side," I said, "we found nearly two bushels of coral—suggesting that it was used as a fluxing-agent. Wouldn't that tend to alkalize the soil?"

"Indeed it would, if the use was extensive. Your Hammersmith friends may have used slag coatings." At my questioning glance, he explained: "This entails a process of heating the finished pieces in beds of mixed charcoal embers and slag. It's an ancient process which provides a protective coating. In India, for instance, there is a famous iron pole many centuries old that hasn't yet shown any sign of rust."

I asked him for his estimate of how fast iron normally deteriorated. "Depending upon conditions, of course, rust corrodes iron at rates varying from .05 to .005 inches a year."

Those figures meant that in three centuries iron as thick as fifteen inches or as thin as one and one-half inches might have disintegrated entirely. Here was another thing about Saugus that was lucky—like the water table that had preserved the tailrace beams and the anvil block. Because the nature of the terrain and soil, we were finding artifacts that might long before have reverted to nature.

That weekend it rained, which helped to make the water-wheel site more easily workable. So on Monday I went to work with spade, putty knife, and trowel in the charcoal-strewn vein. In mid-afternoon I struck wood. Pushing my hands into the freezing, waterlogged earth, I felt the contours of a thin board, and as I scooped away the soil I felt other surfaces, angling off from the first board. The first image that occurred to me was a box, and then, as I cleared away more of the wood, I dared to hope that my dream of finding at least part of the water wheel preserved had come true. I looked down at the ancient saturated boards, gummy with mud; they seemed to form a water-wheel bucket! I dug on until long after darkness closed in and found a three-foot wooden arm extending into the furnace wheelpit; my bucket was twenty inches by fourteen inches by ten inches deep. Even if I found no more, these dimensions could help to establish the size of the wheel which had helped to get this pioneer industry started.

I wanted to know just how the wheel had been buried. It seemed likely that the embankment next to it had been shored up. If this shoring had given way, the wheel might have been buried as it stood. But if, as I was beginning to fear, it had been hap-hazardly dismantled long ago by people in search of boards, there was no telling how little of the skeleton I might uncover.

After photographing the bucket just as I had found it, I had the

The Water Wheel under Central Street

men cut back the soil on the westerly side of the wheel-pit timbers to make digging easier and to minimize slope wash. But by the time I had exposed the bucket along with its spoke, the rain had returned. It was Friday, February 23, before I could work at the site again.

Paul DeMars, my foreman, and his grandson Robert spent the day with me in the pit as we gingerly lifted the newly frost-encrusted earth. Stooped over against an icy wind, we uncovered a second spoke. Lifting out more frozen soil on one side of the spoke, Paul called me to him when he spotted a jagged wooden shape.

"Looks like we got something, Robbie."

"We got a wheel! And more to come! Let's get in on the other side of the spoke." By now it was necessary to use our gasoline pump to free the excavation of the icy subterranean waters that flowed into it. We found a curving piece of wood with the same kind of jagged fracture as in the first find. The distance between these two ends of the wooden semicircle was between twelve and thirteen feet. I thrust my probe rod in at intervals, touching enough of the buried wood to prove that forty per cent of the original circumference of the wheel was still intact. We uncovered oak beams running parallel on either side which had served as the top sills of the water-wheel pit.

"Bob," Paul said to his grandson, "this wheel is the first thing that rolled in America."

Even if that wasn't true, we almost believed it. Our water wheel was so obviously precious that we spent the better part of three months retrieving it from its burial place, working in the cramped and narrow space allowed by the walls of the wheel pit. It developed that this overshot wheel had been fifteen feet ten inches in diameter and had had fifty buckets slanted at fifty degrees to catch a maximum amount of water shooting from above. It was the fill,

The water wheel and its timber-lined pit as it was first exposed.
A gasoline pump was used to drain the underground water that
has preserved the wood.

of course, which had kept the wheel upright. In the initial excavating I found so many boulders that I feared at first that the pieces
of the wheel might have been smashed in the landslide that had
buried it. Yet, except for a few cracks, every piece was intact. My
lucky water table which kept the subterranean ground saturated
had preserved the wheel in a beautiful mud bath.

The floor of the wheel pit was twenty-two and one half feet
below the elevation at which the traffic on Central Street had only
a few months ago whizzed by, completely oblivious of the history
buried below. When the site was excavated entirely, we were able
to get a good look at the oldest water wheel in America, resting in

The Water Wheel under Central Street

almost exactly the position in which it had been turned. Though the hub and the top half of the wheel were gone, the section I'd uncovered was so well preserved that little was left to the imagination. The pit at the wheel's center was twenty-nine inches wide. Glistening from the moisture absorbed from the water table, the ancient wheel was a singular example of colonial craftsmanship. And it had to be preserved.

Knowing nothing of what methods might have been developed in the past, I consulted Frederick Johnson, who several years previously had worked with the Indian fish weirs found under Boylston Street in Boston. Wooden stakes from this excavation, I was told, had been hermetically sealed in an alcohol solution; but our water wheel was much too big for this kind of treatment. I learned that the alum process used in preserving the famous Viking ship found in Gokstad, Norway, had required four years. Dr. H. O'Neill Hencken of the Peabody Museum in Cambridge, Massachusetts, told me of his work with another ancient wooden boat that had been retrieved from the bottom of an Irish pond. A system of dehydrating the wood with alcohol and reconstituting it with wax, he said, had been less than successful.

Perhaps my unique wheel might also have been lost had I not been fortunate in getting together with a biologist, Dr. Elso Barghoorn of Harvard. First testing smaller pieces of wood taken from the wheel pit, Barghoorn found that 87.7 per cent of the content was water. After considerable experiment, we arrived at a method in which each wooden member of the wheel was immersed in specially constructed vats filled with paraffin heated to 245 degrees. As the wet pieces were dropped in they sizzled like French-fried potatoes going into hot grease—as the moisture sizzled out of the wood, the paraffin seeped in to take its place, and when, after about seven hours, the sizzling stopped, the treatment was complete. We found no shrinkage at all in thickness or length, but width decreased by 1.3 degrees. As a result of these methods the wheel and its timbered pit are now on display at the Saugus ironworks museum.

During these years when our physical digging was in progress, Neal Hartley was equally busy searching out-of-the-way archives for any scrap of evidence that would help us interpret our artifacts. It was clear that the wheel had been built from lumber felled on the site of the ironworks, and that much of the construction work had been done by villagers and neighboring farmers. Ancient records came to light to show that as many as one hundred and eighty-five men had worked here in one capacity or another, but of these only thirty-five were real ironworkers. Francis Perry had been the works carpenter, with Richard Hood and John Parker as sawyers, and their skill was amply shown in the wheel preserved

Dr. Elso Barghoorn of Harvard developed a method used successfully in the preservation of the water wheel.

The lower section of the anvil base, preserved by the water table, was found mounted on interlocked beams. After it had been removed from the ground its age was established by counting the rings of the giant tree from which it had been cut.

under Central Street. Nine men were coalers, two were smiths, there were ten doing the highly skilled work of the forge and the rolling- and slitting-mill, and one man, John Francis, was known to have operated the giant iron hammer I'd unearthed. Some of these workers were prisoners taken at Dunbar during the English civil war who had been sent to the colonies as indentured servants. Two of them, at least, were Indians who cut wood for the making of charcoal. As we fitted these historical fragments with the evi-

A ring of iron is still lodged in clay above the base timbers of a
second anvil base.

dence I was finding in the ground, our picture of the works and
its rugged craftsmen became more and more detailed.

These facts about the workers only served to whet my original
interest in Joseph Jenks; and a year and one day after I discovered
the Central Street wheel, while I was working with the crew
spading and going through soils that contained hundreds of metal
pieces, tools, clay pipes, and potsherds, my spade hit an object
which turned out to be the shaft and hub of another water wheel.
My first hope was that it might prove to be Jenks's "engine to go
by water." It was covered by four feet of fill soils and was at least

The Water Wheel under Central Street

6 1

twenty inches above the natural contour which had existed in Jenks's time, indicating that the wheel had been dismantled before it had become buried.

The next week, with Neal Hartley helping me while a heavy snow was falling, I found two sites of water-wheel pits, and within a month a third turned up. The first of these, closest to the furnace, included fifty per cent of an eight-foot overshot wheel, and its shaft and gudgeon-bearing block. The second was a pitchback wheel of approximately the same size. As we sifted the soil in this area downstream from the blast furnace, it revealed more than 1,500 brass common pins, fragments of pipes made from red clay— the first of their kind found north of Jamestown, Virginia—and spoons of various metals, all of which proved to have been manufactured in the seventeenth century.

In late winter and early spring we dug into the Jenks area layer by layer and in the process were able to determine the entire basic pattern of his forge. Because of constant water seepage here, the soil remained soft enough to handle, and my crew chose to work even on the nastiest days. They loved it. There were so many artifacts, so much evidence, that they were just like kids at Christmas. They were finding jew's-harps made as trade items for the Indians and precision tools used by colonial artisans, and the finds kept every hour on the site charged with excitement.

I made the mistake one day of trying to be considerate. One of the men had developed a bad cold, and when I found him warming up over a fire they had built in an oil drum, I decided he'd be better off with an inside job. I told him to go to my office in the museum and clean it up.

I watched him trying to think of something to say.

"What's the matter, Dick? It's warm up there in the building. You want to take it easy with that cold."

"There's nothing to find up there," he said. He picked up his shovel. "Can't let the other guys find all the good stuff. I ain't *that* sick."

In addition to the three water-wheel pits, we found the fulcrum base of the forge hammer, the heating-hearth, and the site where Jenks had kept his charcoal. We also turned up hundreds of leather soles for shoes—perhaps the last stock of an abandoned warehouse that had stood near the Jenks works. Again the water table had minimized deterioration, protecting the leather just as it had the wood.

By the time we hit the Jenks area I had begun to feel at ease in dealing with stratigraphy, principally because this natural amphitheater beside the Saugus River had provided one of the finest training-courses possible. Through careful observation I'd been able to recognize that soil used to build up the low marshy area at the water's edge had been removed from the brow of the amphitheater long before Central Street had been constructed. This fill

The result of the Saugus archaeology is an accurate restoration of water wheels, furnace, forge, and slitting mill as they were originally erected beside the Saugus River in the seventeenth century.

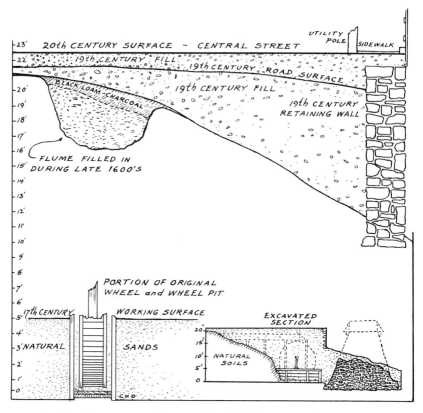

Section showing stratifications found below Central Street, with the water wheel in position at lower left. Inset at lower right shows the wheel in relation to the buried furnace foundation.

was identical with the soil from the slope which had been cut out to make room for the furnace and its water wheel. It isn't often that a single site provides both the fill soil and its source to make recognition so easy. I was also able to observe the rich black topsoil that had gathered about the furnace and to note how rains had washed it down from the heights.

The twenty-two-foot profile we cut beneath Central Street gave us a vivid cross-section of man's ability to change the surface of the earth. In that perpendicular slice I could instantly recognize a buried roadbed which had been laid on what once was topsoil. The road surface was the slimmest of the stratifications, sandwiched between coarse fill and the rich humus that had formed after the wheel had been buried. The profile made obvious two efforts to build up the slope: the lower layer of fill, replete with early American artifacts, had been given time to settle and develop topsoil; on top of this the road had been laid, and sometime later a second layer of fill had accumulated over the road; the final stratification was the surface of Central Street.

I learned that there is no rule, no way of forecasting what specific layers—or how many—there may be when one begins to

Section showing level of water table with part of anvil base preserved below.

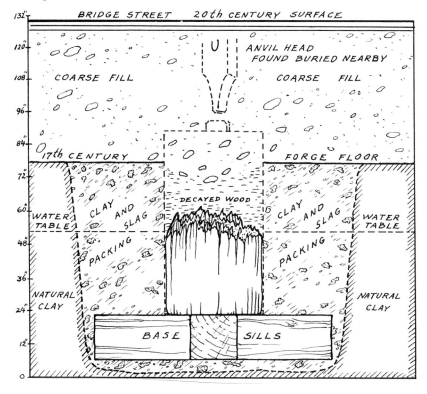

The Water Wheel under Central Street

65

Pewter nipple found at Saugus was used to feed seventeenth-century infants.

A single spoon made of pewter (top), and eight brass spoons were found at Saugus, and identified as seventeenth-century products.

Brass wire was shaped to make this pin found at Saugus.

dig. For practical purposes, there are three types of soil: sands, loams, and clays. We can sink a test pit of given depth at one point and hit natural sand, then dig thirty feet away and at the same depth find natural clay. On the other hand, we might at a third point in the same limited area cut through all three soil conditions. The opportunity provided at Saugus was like a college course in both archaeological and geological stratigraphy.

These ironworks excavations had created a good deal of interest, and I found that we were having visitors from virtually every section of the country. In addition, I had more requests than I could handle to describe the discoveries at the meetings of various organizations. One such appearance was before the neighboring Quincy Historical Society, an engagement that strongly appealed to me because our historical researches had by this time firmly linked "the Company of Undertakers" to the Braintree Ironworks which had existed in what is now West Quincy.

My second venture in excavating an ironworks was the result of this talk I gave in Quincy, but the dig did not take place until two years after the work at Saugus was complete. After correspondence with a number of Quincy citizens, I was called in by the city manager in June 1956. I spent two months uncovering the works that John Winthrop, Jr., had built as the predecessor of the Hammersmith foundry. Winthrop, the man who had gone to England to raise money for "the Company of Undertakers," had picked Braintree as the site of the first ironworks in New England. For two years before he settled in Connecticut—of which he later was to be governor—he struggled with the problems of the infant industry, and then withdrew in favor of Richard Leader, who in turn moved on to Saugus.

I had sunk a number of test holes at Quincy in the winter of 1953, determining that at least a part of the furnace still remained. When the dig began in earnest we had to clear the site not only

The Water Wheel under Central Street

of weeds, brush, and small trees, but also of rusty cans, broken bottles, and other refuse abandoned there. Beneath this rubbish we found a layer of gravel and sandy soil from a foot to twenty inches in depth which had been thrown here when a near-by road was built a century earlier. Working with pick-mattocks, shovels, trowels, putty knives, whiskbrooms, the ever-present probe rod, in addition to a small bulldozer and a mechanical back hoe, we found the ruined furnace buried at depths ranging from two and a half feet to ten feet. Twenty-three feet square at its base, the furnace was only slightly smaller than the one at Saugus and its construction of dry-laid fieldstones was almost identical with its neighbor's.

It was a much smaller operation, however, suggesting nothing of the integrated assembly line that Leader had conceived at Hammersmith. Our digging laid bare the casting-beds for both pig iron and hollow ware, and we uncovered the site of a single water wheel, although the wheel itself had long vanished. The most interesting discovery we made was an intricate furnace-draining system, an engineering feat that added meaningfully to notes in John Winthrop, Jr.'s handwriting found among the family papers; young Winthrop had copied down the advice he had received from an English friend: "Cheefely take care so to place your furnasse," Winthrop had written, "that there be noe water springs or dampness under hir for it will spoile all which if your ground will not admitt you must make a false bottom with several pipes to carry away the dampness and water or springs."

"The false bottom with several pipes" at the Braintree works proved to be an arrangement of subterranean stone channels which drew off all moisture from the danger of contact with molten

ABOVE   Ruins of the second blast furnace unearthed at Quincy.

BELOW   Conjectural drawing of blast furnace at Quincy shows the water wheel which gave it power and the charging-bridge over which the ore was carried.

John Winthrop, Jr
BLAST FURNACE
1644

metal. This problem had been solved at Hammersmith through the simple use of slope drainage running into the furnace tailrace, but the Braintree engineering has more interest, at least archaeologically speaking. At this site in West Quincy there still remains the earliest tangible evidence of this kind of colonial enterprise. Here, a century before the War of Jenkins's Ear and one hundred and thirty years before the Boston Tea Party, American industry, smoking and belching as earnestly as it does today in Bethlehem or Pittsburgh, had been born.

A century and a half before the Revolutionary War is a long time in American history; the era of the Hammersmith ironworks must have seemed as ancient to the signers of the Declaration of Independence as their historic meetings seem to us today. Our excavations, rewarding as they were, touched only one phase of the life of that time. Other phases, other details of everyday New England life in this resourceful era are still to be recognized—underground.

4

Jefferson's Legacy Underground

I<small>T HAS BEEN SAID</small> that archaeology, as a science, began in America. The distinguished Sir Mortimer Wheeler, former director of the University of London's Institute of Archaeology, has identified that beginning in Jefferson's skillful excavation and recording of his finds at the Indian burial mound near Monticello. "Let us consider," Wheeler writes,[1] "the contents of Jefferson's clear and concise report. He describes the situation of the mound in relation to natural features and evidence of human occupation. He detects components of geological interest in its materials and traces their sources. He indicates the stratigraphical stages in the construction of the mound. He records certain significant features of the skeletal remains. And he relates his evidence objectively to current theories. No mean achievement for a busy statesman in

[1] Sir Mortimer Wheeler: *Archaeology from the Earth.*

1784!" And Wheeler goes on: "Unfortunately, this seed of a new scientific skill fell upon infertile soil. For a century after Jefferson, mass-excavation remained the rule of the day."

Even the spectacular discoveries made by Heinrich Schliemann at Troy were haphazard and almost criminally unscientific. Men were slow to learn that much of history can be deciphered from careful study of the earth itself as well as from the gaudy artifacts it may contain. Perhaps Jefferson was the first to fully understand the value of stratigraphy. He dug into his mound to eliminate conjecture, to find out as much as he could about why and how these Indian bones had been covered with earth.

"I first dug superficially in several parts of it," he said in *Notes on Virginia*, "and came to collections of human bones, at different depth, from six inches to three feet below the surface. These were lying in the utmost confusion, some vertical, some oblique, some horizontal, and directed to every point of the compass, entangled and held together in clusters by the earth." He noted that small bones of the feet were found in the hollows of skulls, that no complete skeleton was found, and that the only white bone was a fragment of a child's jaw; all others were sand-colored. "I proceeded then to make a perpendicular cut through the body of the barrow, that I might examine its internal structure. . . . At the bottom, that is, on the level of the circumjacent plain, I found bones; above these a few stones, brought from a cliff a quarter of a mile off; then a large interval of earth, then a stratum of bones, and so on. . . . The bones nearest the surface were least decayed. No holes were discovered in any of them, as if made with bullets, arrows, or other weapons."

Thus Jefferson provided a system, the essentials of which are still used today, for examining buried history. Realizing that he was an amateur archaeologist just as I had been and that his system was basically the same as the one I had evolved by trial and error, I felt a real kinship tor Mr. Jefferson.

I made my first trip to the plantation called Shadwell on November 8, 1954. In company with Raymond Hunt, a member of the Thomas Jefferson Birthplace Memorial Park Commission, and Floyd Johnson, the Commission's architect, I drove the four miles east from Charlottesville, Virginia, to the rolling Piedmont land that lies between the Rivanna River and Route 250. We turned off on the winding dirt road that climbs from the highway to a grove that had sheltered a late-nineteenth-century house torn down by the Commission the previous year. There were still eleven ramshackle outbuildings in and adjacent to the grove, and beyond it was a field sweeping east and south to the river. In this area, on the cold morning of February 1, 1770, a Virginia gentleman's home had been consumed by fire; it was the house in which the author of the Declaration of Independence had been born.

Two expeditions had been here before me. In 1941 several foundations had been excavated on the edge of the field, and in 1954 test trenches had been run into the grove, to determine if there had been any previous occupation at the site of the house which the Commission tore down. In neither of these digs had the interpretation of evidence of the birthplace site been conclusive. As a result, I had volunteered to make a survey.

I spent a day covering the area on foot, plunging my probe rod in at intervals to determine whether artifacts of timber, stone, or brick still existed. On the next day my interest was narrowed to the ridge extending easterly from the grove for almost 100 yards. The crest of this land was surprisingly level, averaging more than one hundred feet in width, and in its widest part spread north and south for somewhat more than one hundred and thirty feet. Here was a commanding view to the north, east, and south, with the Rivanna flowing gently past the fall-away of land on the south. On the west was the grove; it had not existed during the occupa-

Jefferson's Legacy Underground

tion by Peter Jefferson, father of the President, and had only to be removed to afford a fine view of Monticello, on the hilltop two miles away. Standing on this crest, I could easily imagine how the sight of that hilltop had set young Tom Jefferson to dream of one day building his own house on that piece of his father's land. Perhaps he might even have studied that view from the veranda of the house in which he was born.

On my third day of survey my probe rod struck brick, and as I went to work, first with a shovel, then with putty knife and broom, I uncovered a solid shape of bricks which, I was now told, had been exposed in 1941—described then as "a hearth definitely hollowed at the top." I sank my probe rod between the bricks and discovered that the soil beneath was fill, a fact which had not been learned in the previous digs. I carefully removed the brick "hearth" and found below a layer of red clay which seemed natural—as if it had never been disturbed by man. Actually it covered a deposit of black soil in which I found evidence of charcoal and numerous artifacts. Further digging revealed a structure four feet square with walls of a single layer of ancient brick and, thirty-two inches below the ground level, a floor of clay that had been beaten to a hard surface. Obviously an affair so superficially constructed was not intended to support the sills of any structure; it was apparent that this was a small pit which had been lined with brick to keep it clean, and sunk into the earth under the shelter of a good-sized building. Perhaps it had served as a cooling-cellar for wines or other liquids, and was reached by a trap door in the floor above.

Although the earth I removed from the pit contained charcoal and layers of earth blackened by fire, I could tell at once that the fill did not consist solely of the debris of a flaming house. The pit had been buried considerably after the fire, for the fill contained refuse collected from various parts of the plantation. There were, for instance, many unburned animal bones. There were also pieces

Bricks that may have been made on the Jefferson plantation were used to line one of the small cooling-cellars we unearthed.

of earthenware intermixed with clay pipe fragments which later examination proved to have been manufactured earlier than the Jefferson fire. Out of this hole I took a bone-handled knife and a fork, an inkwell, fragments of old window glass, a pewter spoon, metal buckles, pieces of hand-painted Staffordshire and cream-ware, salt glaze, 399 hand-made nails and a good-sized piece of a kettle or pan. Nearly a pound of plaster or mortar fragments was also removed.

I was not able to prove that any of these items had ever been used by the Peter Jefferson family, but the evidence I turned up in that survey made it advisable to have a systematic excavation of the area surrounding the small cellar. Accordingly I came back in April, 1955, having spent a good deal of time during the winter

Jefferson's Legacy Underground

pursuing the written record of Jefferson's life at Shadwell. A paragraph from Henry Randall's biography, written eighty years after the fire, had stuck in my mind:

"A little more than a mile from [the Rivanna's] eastern outlet, on one of those gentle swells into which the river banks are here everywhere broken—in the midst of a new cultivated field—stand two plane trees and two locust trees; and hard by is a cavity, nearly filled by the plow, indicating to the passer, by bits of broken bricks and plaster, and remnants of chimney-stones, fire-cracked and vitrified, which lay in and about it, that here had once been a cellar of a human habitation. A Virginia farm-house formerly occupied the site. It was of a story and a half in height; had the four spacious ground rooms and hall, with garret chambers above, common in those structures a hundred years since; and also the huge outside chimneys, planted against the Gothic buttresses, but massive enough, had such been their use, to support the walls of a cathedral, instead of those of a low wooden cottage. In that

Section showing how bit of post-hole digger cut through plowed surface at Shadwell.

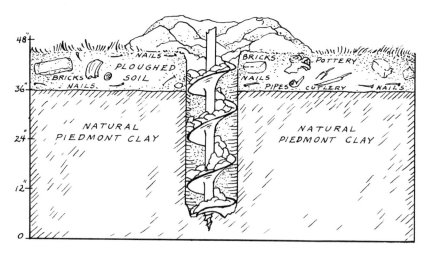

One of the small cellars was simply a rectangle cut into the hard-packed Piedmont clay, without walls of any kind.

house was born Thomas Jefferson; the plane and locust trees were planted by his hand on his twenty-first birthday."

To what extent the biographer had exercised poetic license I did not yet know, but—with the exception of the plane and locust trees, which no longer stood—I could imagine that description fitting the area in which I proposed to work. Here on the ridge where I had dug in the fall, Floyd Johnson had had engineers stake out a ten-foot grid pattern to facilitate plotting. The grid covered more than an acre of the land I proposed to take apart piece by piece, if necessary, in an effort to find what remained of Peter Jefferson's homestead. My first move was to hire a tractor with a post-hole digger attachment to punch a hole at each of the 576 stakes that marked off the grid. It was a little like prospecting for oil. We could drill, but there was no assurance we would hit a

Jefferson's Legacy Underground

gusher—even in archaeological terms. Yet because the holes were fourteen inches in diameter and thirty-six to forty inches in depth, I was getting a look at the stratification at almost six hundred intervals, examination of which would quickly tell the depth of cultivation and other man-made disturbances. Many eighteenth century Virginia houses did not have foundation cellars, but had there been one for the Jefferson house my post holes would tell me, either by revealing the walls themselves or the subterranean vestiges they had left.

My archaeological wells immediately showed that in more than an acre of land there was no sign of a cellar the size of a house. In general the ridge soils had been disturbed only to a depth of eight inches—the result of years of cultivating tobacco and other crops. Below the level of the plowshare was nothing but natural Piedmont clay, untouched by the hand of man.

However, at stake M32 the big drill was stopped at that eight-inch level. I scraped away the churned soil with my putty knife and found a flat stone. Probing carefully with the rod, I could outline a six-foot-long oval shape which I excavated with the spade. Swept free of soil, it turned out to be a layer of bricks and stones— perhaps a rude hearth. Whatever might be disclosed by thorough study, the rough structure was further evidence of ancient habitation at this particular spot on the Shadwell acres.

Merely to have found even so crude a foundation that had escaped notice in previous excavations had its satisfaction, but the real challenge was to sift from this much-tilled soil every fragmentary clue that might in some way help to describe the frame structure in which Jefferson had grown up. So far the most important evidence was negative. Because there was no full-scale cellar to help us imagine how large the dwelling had been, and

Piles of brick fragments, each found within a single grid square, helped to locate the site of the Peter Jefferson house.

because whatever footings the house had had were destroyed either by the fire itself or by generations of plowing, there was no chance of turning up the kind of tangible evidence that had been preserved at the Saugus ironworks. Here there was no lucky water table to preserve Jefferson timbers. My best hope was to locate artifacts that could be conclusively tied to the Jefferson occupation. I set to work chasing down every elusive clue.

This involved painstakingly shaving down the rectangles I'd staked out, each of which was ten feet square. Each square was recorded by its four stake numbers and assigned an additional number designating the chronological order in the shaving process; any and all artifacts found within the square were deposited in a large paper bag correspondingly numbered and dated.

After breaking the soil apart, the workmen sifted it with their hands as each spadeful went into a wheelbarrow. In the spring sunlight bits of charcoal stood out like black diamonds in the red earth; each was a dead ember of a fire—a fire that on the first day of February 1770 "deprived Mr. Jefferson of the books and papers of his early life . . . He wrote Page that he lost 'every paper he had in the world, and almost every book.' He said the cost of the books burned was equal to two hundred pounds sterling, and he 'would to God it had been the money, and then it would have cost me never a sigh' . . . Mr. Jefferson used to tell, in after years, with great glee, an anecdote connected with his fire. He was absent from home when it occurred, and a slave arrived out of breath to inform him of the disaster. After learning the general destruction, he inquired; 'But were none of my books saved?' 'No, master', was the reply, 'but' (with a look of truly African satisfaction), 'we saved the fiddle!' "[2]

This charcoal we were finding was all that remained of Jeffer-

_____

[2] Henry Randall: *Life of Jefferson.*

Foundations of two dependency buildings were found buried not far from the area (background) containing the scattered brick.

son's early library. But, futile as these deposits of carbon were in this sense, we were also sifting out more tangible artifacts which could be related both to the house that Jefferson's father had built and to the occupation of the family of Craven Peyton, to whom Jefferson in 1799 had leased the property, including an unknown number of buildings. In this earth so often turned over by the plow we found 9,106 nails, of which roughly ninety per cent were hand-made, still showing the irregular edges caused by the colonial chisels which had shaped them out of bar iron. We turned up more than 400 pieces of ancient window glass, and 3,000 other specimens included sherds of porcelain, pottery, and bottle glass. There were metal buckles from colonial shoes, eighteenth-century iron knives and forks with bone handles. A nineteenth-century pewter

Jefferson's Legacy Underground

plate, undamaged by time, lay just below the bite of the plow blade.

Cautiously, I dug into the soil below the crude oval shape of bricks and stone at Stake M32. In the one-and-a-half-inch layer of disturbed soil that lay immediately under this foundation I discovered eleven handmade nails, eleven fragments of green bottle, fifteen pieces of window glass, five earthenware sherds, one of pottery, a piece of a clam shell, six pieces of bone, one animal tooth—and the inevitable charcoal. Careful study of the bricks used in the foundation showed that they had seen service before in some other construction, for one piece had smooth mortar still clinging on its bottom side. The fact that so many artifacts were found underneath the base made it quite clear that the stones and bricks had been set in the earth after the fire.

So far, in spite of finding so much that had eluded other diggers, we had nothing that could be associated beyond the shadow of a doubt with Jefferson's boyhood. I was convinced by this time that the birthplace had stood on the very spot at which my crew was working, but the combination of the fire and subsequent cultivation had either destroyed or scattered the outlines of the building, which might otherwise have been recognizable underground.

I drove sixty-five miles down Route 250 to Tuckahoe, the plantation on which Jefferson had lived from his fifth to his twelfth year and which his father had operated for the widow of William Randolph, Peter Jefferson's closest friend. Here I hoped to find new clues to the kind of house the senior Jefferson must have built, for the Tuckahoe mansion still stands and it was of the same vintage as the lost Shadwell dwelling.

In Jefferson's time the area through which I drove had been as much the West as Montana is today, for settlement ended then just over the mountains. Here the elegant architecture of coastal Virginia was lacking. Private buildings were, Jefferson says in his

Notes, "very rarely constructed of stone or brick, much the greatest portion being of scantling and boards, plastered with lime. It is impossible to devise things more ugly, uncomfortable, and happily more perishable." The Piedmont colonists were still in buckskin, wearing Indian moccasins and coonskin caps. "The poorest people build huts of logs, laid horizontally in pens, stopping the interstices with mud," Jefferson wrote.

But Peter Jefferson was far from poor. He owned more than a thousand acres at Shadwell, and another vast tract at Snowden. Though he lacked formal education, he was a surveyor who with Joshua Fry made the first accurate map of Virginia; he was a magistrate, a member of the House of Burgesses, and it is recorded that by the light of a log fire he was wont to read Shakespeare, Swift, and Addison to his family. "Scantling and boards" his house may have been, in accordance with contemporary styles, but this man who had married the daughter of one of Virginia's most distinguished families, whose close associates were the colony's most influential men, was likely to have erected a substantial dwelling.

The probability that his house had been similar in design and structure to the Tuckahoe mansion moved me to look closely at the way the latter had been set into the earth. I found a handsome building which had been built in two sections, both of them two-and-a-half stories high. The older wing, dating to the period of Peter Jefferson's construction, was without a cellar but was supported by a stone foundation set into the ground. Well preserved as it is, it is just as perishable as Jefferson pointed out. Had this Tuckahoe wing burned to the ground as Shadwell had, it too might have left few clues to its location. For as I used a probe rod to pry under the foundation stones, I found that the footings averaged between twenty and twenty-three inches in depth. Although this seemed to conflict with the fact that at Shadwell I was finding untouched soil at eight inches below the surface, there were two

important considerations. According to memories considered reliable, the Shadwell house had been only one-and-a-half stories and therefore would not need footings so deeply set. In addition, and more important to me, I was sure that considerable erosion had occurred at Shadwell as the result of the numerous plowings of that high, wind-swept land.

To verify this deduction, I enlisted a government soil-study team. These experts determined that all of the original topsoil at Shadwell had been removed by nature, along with some of the subsoil, thus bringing the level down ten to twenty inches from what it had been in Jefferson's time. The knowledge of this loss of earth removed the last hope of identifying dimensional outlines of any structure built almost two hundred years before.

Winds from the Blue Ridge mountains, sweeping across the Piedmont, had slowly but surely whipped away soil, loosened by the plow, on which the Shadwell house had stood. Had grass grown over this site, it would have held erosion to a minimum; a green carpet might have sealed in the rotting timbers of the house's sills, or protected other clues that could have told us much of what we wanted to know about the birthplace. But it was clear now that wind and rain and the repeated tilling of tobacco and other crops had spirited away the evidence that would have made any archaeologist's task easier. I had now to depend upon the artifacts that had escaped the plow.

Early in May, as we shaved down grid square 23, one of the men shook out a heavy object from his spade. It was clearly metal, heavily encrusted with clay, and had the general appearance of a battered brick. Cleaning it down with a soft brush I began to see traces of a fine design. First I made out a talon, then a leaping

All that remains of the superintendent's house at Tuckahoe plantation. Cows, hungry for calcium, licked away mortar to cause the appearance of erosion at the base.

Conjectural sketch of the Jefferson fireback design. Shaded area indicates the fragment identified by experts in heraldry.

beast, then two animals with tails. The outer surface on which the design was embossed showed beyond doubt that it had been subjected to heat for long periods. What was it? I picked up a second piece sifted out of the earth in grid square 21 and found its design less distinct. Yet if these pieces had once been part of a whole, they might have formed a fireback, the ornamented slabs of cast iron once used to protect the backs of fireplaces.

Soon afterward I drove to Brookline, Massachusetts, to have the larger piece examined by Dr. Harold Bowditch, a member of the College of Heraldry, and a well-known authority on coats of arms.

Sitting in Dr. Bowditch's study, I waited a moment as he turned the ancient metal in his hand.

"At first glance," he said, "there seems no doubt that the design here is part of the Royal Shield of Great Britain. In its entirety, it is a quartered circle rather than in the shape of a shield. What you've identified as a talon is the claw of the Lion of Britain. And just above the circle is the beginning of the helmet that crowned the device." From the bookshelves he took down a copy of *Display of Heraldry*, published in 1632. My "leaping beast," he pointed out, was one of three passant leopards. He began to sketch the Shield of Great Britain, and showed me the differences between the design under Queen Anne's reign and that of the Hanovers who were in power during the last eighty-six years of the eighteenth century. My fragment of the upper left quarter corresponded with both.

"Can we establish to which of the reigns the Shadwell piece belongs?"

"The break down the middle makes it impossible to be sure," Dr. Bowditch said. "Yet in either event it falls into a period contemporary with Thomas Jefferson's birth."

In the years after the Revolutionary War and the rejection by Americans of all things related to English royalty, there was no chance that a regal design would have been built into a new house. Even if Craven Peyton had put up a dwelling after he leased the property in 1799—ten years after Washington's inauguration—this royal fireback would not have been a part of it. There was now every reason to believe that the battered metal pieces, so long buffeted by plows, had survived the fire of 1770 after decorating the fireplace in the house Peter Jefferson had erected while the colonies were still loyal.

Digging is often a one-man job and satisfying because it is, but analysis and interpretation require the fresh eye and coolly objective approach of many outsiders—the more the better. Just as I felt the need of a specialist's interpretation of the fireback, I wanted to consult H. Geiger Omwake, who had given me a good deal of advice on the first clay pipes I had found at Saugus. I sent Geiger a small lot from Shadwell which included two complete pipe bowls, three specimens having portions of the bowl and stem, and one unmarked stem fragment.

He placed these pipes as having been manufactured, probably in Holland, in the period in which Jefferson was born. In his conclusion, he said: "Because all six items were found in association and under the same conditions and because they exhibit features which compare favorably with those known and assumed to have been in vogue during the first half of the eighteenth century, it is felt that all six specimens may be attributed to that period and probably, because of the similarity of bowl shape to other pipes whose period of manufacture, based on the dating of associated materials, has been determined to have been between 1720 and 1740 . . . it is felt that all six examples probably occurred toward the latter part of the first half of the eighteenth century, possibly 1725-1750."

I now had further reason to be convinced that this was the site of the Peter Jefferson house. The pipes had been caught in the debris of the fire and had been raked into the mixture of soil and charcoal which filled the small brick-lined pit and a second similar cooling-cellar we unearthed not far from the first.

As the hot sun of the summer solstice burned down I began to marshal my findings for assessment. In an area one hundred and thirty feet east of the grove that now obscures the view of Monticello, we had found the heavy concentration of fire evidence—charcoal, the fireback fragments, hand-cut nails, and early-eighteenth-century clay pipes, window glass, potsherds, china, eating-utensils, and thousands of pieces of early brick. Here Peter Jefferson had lived with his wife, the former Jane Randolph, and his nine children, seven of whom lived beyond infancy. Here, on this table-flat red earth, Thomas Jefferson had learned to walk, dreamed of building for himself on his "little mountain" to the west, gazed out toward the Blue Ridge where the wilderness began. Here had stood the house in which the President had been born.

What kind of house was it? It was a frame house, mortise-and-tenoned and secured with thousands of nails chiseled from iron by hand. Not so grand as Henry Randall imagined, it was probably one-and-a-half stories high with at least one brick chimney. Certainly it was commodious—for it gave shelter to nine members of

Map of part of Jefferson's Shadwell holdings is believed to have been drawn by him about the time he leased plantation.

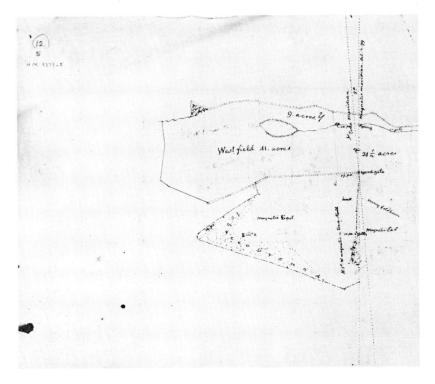

Jefferson's Legacy Underground

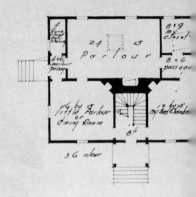

Plan for restoration of Jefferson birthplace,

a family highly regarded socially. The house rose from the ground around the two small cooling-cellars, and when it was consumed by fire, some of the ashes and charred wood settled in these pits which once had been entered through trap doors in the floor. Our digging—especially under the oval foundation—made it clear that after this disaster to the birthplace, a second dwelling had been erected on the same site, perhaps for the widow of Peter Jefferson or for the Peyton family who lived on the property for thirteen years after Thomas had established himself at Monticello.

Before the fire the Jeffersons had one frame outbuilding one hundred feet east of the homestead and under it was a third small cellar hole for cooling or storage purposes; about the same distance west I uncovered the brick-walled basement of a second outbuilding, and beyond it the stone foundation of another dependency shed. The house and the two flanking structures were lined up perfectly, following the established pattern in Piedmont Virginia. The evidence our tools had exposed made it possible to visualize these colonial buildings standing proudly on this crest above the

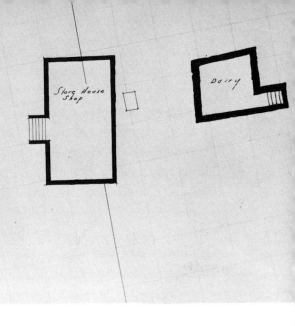

based on archaeological evidence.

Rivanna River much the way that Mount Vernon overlooks the Potomac.

The digging possibilities at Shadwell are by no means exhausted, for the site of Peter Jefferson's mill on the edge of the river is untouched, and there are numerous dependency buildings mentioned in the Jefferson account books which time didn't permit me to explore. I left Shadwell in July to go on to a dig at one of the early Dupont powder-mill sites in Delaware.

In April, 1956 I got a call from the Thomas Jefferson Memorial Foundation to do an archaeological survey at Monticello. Buried here on the site to which Jefferson moved shortly after the Shadwell fire were the foundations of several buildings apparently torn down after ownership passed from the Jefferson family. On the afternoon before the President's 213th birthday I drove up the "little mountain" and began using my probe rod in the area back of the house where it was believed a nailery, a servant's house, a cider room, a rum cellar, a saw bit, a joiner's shop, and a weaver's cottage had once stood. To accurately restore this part of the

Jefferson's Legacy Underground

estate, the Commission had asked for as much information as could be determined without extensive excavations. Almost immediately my probe rod was striking slag. Test trenching showed that four to eight inches of burned soil covered a stone floor. In an area eighteen feet by thirty-eight and one-half feet I found the clear dimensions of the nailery building, now covered with earth containing charcoal from the heating-hearth, nails and bar iron from which the nails were cut, and forge scoria so heavy with iron waste that a magnet would pick up the clinkers. I found outlines of other buildings east and west of the nailery, and thus, simple though this survey had been, I was able to help the Commission identify beyond doubt the true site for their proposed restoration of Jefferson's nail-making shop.

5

The Philipse Dynasty: Court Baron on the Tappan Zee

SIXTY YEARS before Jefferson was born, a shrewd Dutch merchant built a house of stone at a point where the Pocantico River flows into the Hudson. His barony stretched eight miles eastward to the Bronx River, and ran some thirty miles north and south—from the Croton River to the Harlem. It was a domain as large as Andorra, Monaco, and San Marino all rolled into one, a sparsely settled tract still covered with primeval vegetation. This Dutchman, pledged to the English reign of William and Mary, was Frederick Philipse, founder of a commercial and social dynasty that was to center on these lands for almost one hundred years.

By the autumn of 1956, when I first surveyed the site, all but the old stone house was gone. An automobile plant filled the mouth of a Hudson River bay that once had welcomed Philipse ships; the

Seventeenth-century Dutch clearing land.

harbor was now dry land. The vast domain had been cut to twenty acres, covered with layers of earth added one after the other by the sequence of owners who had succeeded the dynasty. So diligently had the terrain been built up that what had been the ground floor of the house was now the basement. Equally buried, I knew, were whatever vestiges remained of Frederick Philipse's mill and river-yard—among the oldest surviving ruins of the first settlement of the Hudson Valley. It was a site that would take me back again to the seventeenth century, to the beginnings of Colonial commerce, and to an environment that had shaped the characteristic American drive to amass great fortunes. It was to be the first major archaeological investigation of the Dutch period in New York.

Philipse had been a self-made man. Before 1650 he had landed at New Amsterdam in the company of his mother, intent upon making his way as a carpenter. With Peter Stuyvesant as one of his clients, he made steady progress. As the Dutch colonies thrived —growing from 2,000 to 10,000 in the ten years beginning in 1653—so did he. In 1657 he was made a small burgher, with the right to hold minor municipal offices and engage in trade. By 1660, when he was thirty-four, he had chartered a sloop of the Dutch West India Company for a mercantile expedition to Virginia. Later he extended his trading activities to the upper Hudson Valley. In 1662 he married the extremely wealthy Margaret Hardenbrook de Vries, a widow who herself was very active in the shipping business; and by 1674—not yet fifty—Frederick Philipse was listed as the richest man in the New York colony.

Philipse Castle in 1866.

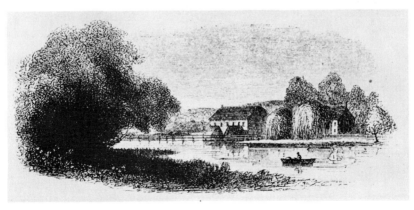

The Philipse Dynasty

95

The dam and mill in 1866.

Though the settlement which Philipse so dominated commercially was being hacked out of the wilderness, his ships were well known in the most civilized harbors of the Old World. There are records of their calls at Hamburg, London, and Bristol, at Amsterdam and Madagascar, Texel, St. Helena, the Isle of Wight. They carried the appurtenances of gracious living to Americans, and some of them dropped anchor in the Bight of Benin to fill their holds with slaves from the Guinea coast.

Not far from where his ships sometimes docked in New York harbor, Philipse had acquired one piece of property after another; at one point he owned six houses within the city. In this era the city was so thoroughly Dutch that a traveler who wandered from the wooden palisades on Wall Street, past the wharves or along the canal, might have imagined himself in a town of old Holland. Philipse and his fellow burghers had created a community marked by curving streets and a skyline studded with black and red tile roofs that often ended in gables notched like steps. The roofs of New York were almost as vivid as those of Amsterdam and Delft. Houses were made of yellow, black, red, and blue bricks sometimes laid in checkered patterns, or of native quarried stone. Little is known of Philipse's taste in architecture, but there is little reason to doubt that he was a canny, and always conservative, exemplar

Headless Horseman Bridge.

The Philipse Dynasty

97

of the burgher tradition. He seems to have applied the craftsmanship of the trade for which he was trained to everything he did in
his years of affluence. He was a contemporary of De Peysters, Van
Cortlandts, Van Vechtens, Steenwycks, and Roosevelts. His city
life was the life of a politically oriented man of affairs, a man with
influence on local business and local society, one whose prestige
was noted wherever the running streams and oceans carried his
vessels.

The principal stream in the life of Frederick Philipse was the
Hudson. When he built his stone house on its banks in 1683, there
was little successful settlement between Manhattan and Albany—
the mecca for merchants like Philipse who traded in furs. Of five
patroonships established in 1629 to promote the growth of the
colony, only Rensselaerwyck survived. With the Indians moving
westward in pursuit of the pelts coveted by Europeans, the valley
remained largely unpopulated until the English, at the end of the
seventeenth century, established successful merchants as lords of
manors. Frederick Philipse was one of these. Beside his house and
mill he organized a small but busy port, and workers came to settle
and to help him tame the wilderness.

The demesne that comprised the western third of Westchester
County received a Royal Charter as the "Manor of Philipsborough,"
and the man who had sailed from Bolswaert, Friesland, as a carpenter some forty years before was given the right to preside over
Court Baron and Court Leet, retaining "all fines, issues and
amercements," and to serve as the manor's arbiter of justice. He
had the right to mine, except for gold and silver, the right of
patronage over all and every church on manor lands, the right to
erect a bridge across the Harlem and to charge toll for its use. For
all this, and more, he paid £4 12s a year, less than the average
tenant paid for the privilege of tilling a few acres. As a bolster to
his cannily won commercial success he served as a member of the

governor's council from 1680 until the year before his death in 1702.

Some of his contemporaries accused him of "great concerns in illegal trade," and in a letter written from Albany in 1698, the Earl of Bellomont reported in some frustration: "They write from New Yorke that Arabian Gold is in great plenty there. When Frederick Phillipps' ship and the two other come from Madagascar (which are expected every day) New York will abound with gold. 'Tis the most beneficiall trade, that to Madagascar with the pirates, that was ever heard of, and I believe there's more got that way than by turning pirates and robbing."

We have yet to find real proof that Frederick Philipse knew more about pirates than other New Yorkers of the time, for it was a period when freebooters were as welcome as any in New York waters. Certainly there has been no sign of an illicit treasure trove in the excavations beside his house; only a few coins have turned up, and these bear the likeness of George II, who didn't reign until Philipse had been dead a quarter-century.

Philipse's will cut the estate in two. His son Adolph took over the establishment on the Pocantico—called Philipsburg Manor, Upper Mills—and a grandson, Frederick, sometime between 1716 and 1719 ensconced himself in the southern manorial seat at Yonkers. Thirty-odd years later, after Adolph had followed his father's career as both a free-wheeling trader and government official, Frederick Philipse II reunited the two halves. His Tory son, Frederick III, was driven to England in 1783. As a result, part of the Upper Manor of Philipsburg was sold to the Gerard Beekman family, who stayed for more than half a century. Steadily diminishing in size, the grounds around the stone house still managed to attract distinguished proprietors. The house became the country

Stone house and mill pond in twentieth century. Mill building at left was torn down in 1959 to make way for further excavation.

seat of Ambrose Kingsland, mayor of New York in the 1850's, and after World War I it was the suburban residence of Elsie Janis, the "sweetheart of the A.E.F." Each changed the land as he saw fit, burying old structures, studding the Philipse soil with new ones. We were to find as many as five distinct building levels on one foundation. Not until after 1940, when John D. Rockefeller, Jr., made funds available, was there opportunity for a restoration that would accurately convey the flavor of Dutch colonial life to the twentieth century.

Ever since I had heard about it, I had been interested in the Philipse site, yet it was not until mid-summer of 1956 that I was able to consider digging here. The research director of Sleepy Hollow Restorations, which owns the site, had first turned to Colonial Williamsburg, then to the National Park Service for advice on archaeologists with experience at historic sites. Both efforts led him to me as I was about to finish the blast-furnace excavation at Quincy. Toward the end of July, I drove down to Tarrytown to discuss possibilities, and on September 4 I was on the grounds ready to begin a three-month survey.

There is no doubt in my mind that what I looked at that day was the most beautiful segment of landscape I'll ever be asked to ravage with archaeological tools. Canadian geese and mallard ducks cruised in the motionless mill pond just off the old Albany post road, and behind was the handsome stone house, framed by willows and locusts. This was Sleepy Hollow country, where, the story goes, the Headless Horseman had encountered Ichabod Crane crossing this very mill stream. A wooden foot bridge led across the great boulders of the mill dam, and water spilled in silver splashes from the wheel beside a reproduction of an early mill. The lawns and gardens were so nicely kept that I hated the thought of cutting into them.

The Philipse house, long called Philipse Castle in spite of a total absence of turrets and crenelated parapets, had been open to the public for more than a decade. The house had been carefully refurbished to suggest the atmosphere of the Dutch period on the Hudson. The challenge I was offered in 1956 was to assess the archaeological potential—without interrupting the visitors' program—as a new phase of the continuing restoration.

Three months is ample time for such a survey no matter how meager or abundant the potential. The purpose always is the same: to dig only enough to determine the extent of underground relics. Sinking test holes at various logical points in the terrain might have proved that the contours had been so often disarranged that there would be no practical value in a full-scale excavation designed to restore the site to its appearance during the Philipse occupancy. On the other hand, such test holes can—as they did in the fall and early winter of 1956—reveal sufficient signs of habitation to justify digging until all the evidence is unearthed.

As I examined the handsome setting surrounding the Philipse house—the water-powered grist mill, the architecturally accurate reconstruction of a slave house, the eighteenth-century Dutch barn—I realized that many visitors to Tarrytown would question the need for archaeology. The house itself was unimpeachable evidence of early Dutch life. The other structures seemed authentic enough to satisfy the average curiosity about the beginnings of America. Why dig?

Why? Because, as other archaeologists are still proving at Williamsburg, history as represented by the written word can often be both inaccurate and open to misinterpretation. Many buildings of nineteenth- and twentieth-century origin were torn down at Williamsburg in order to find the foundations of houses built by the first settlers. In many cases, the ensuing finds corrected mistaken notions about colonial society which up to then had been based only on letters or incomplete contemporary reports.

The Philipse Dynasty

In Tarrytown, the historical record of the Philipse family had been meager indeed, yet the avowed intent was to make Philipsburg Manor the most accurate representation possible of the years of the Dutch domination in the Hudson. Without digging there would be no chance at all of achieving such accuracy. In order to learn as much as possible about how ships were docked in this wilderness reach of the river, about what kinds of items were traded with the Indians, and what were the earliest milling methods in Westchester County, we would have to dig for the tangible evidence buried under layers of soil.

Suburban Tarrytown surrounds the twenty acres on which the stone house is located. A twentieth-century wall dikes the Pocantico River. The mill dam was built in the nineteenth century. Where a manufacturing plant today sprawls so substantially between the house and the Tappan Zee, ocean-going ships once furled their sails. It seems difficult to realize that man, even with Nature's help, would spend the energy in filling and building up so large an area. Yet maps and written words indicated that this purposeful change occurred, and archaeology could tell us exactly

Section showing how area beside Philipse house was built up.

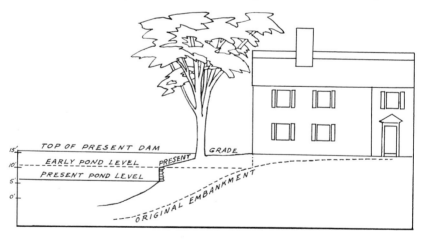

where that buried harbor bottom existed as well as the dimensions of the first structures built on its shores. The exposure of these things would make possible a restoration of the scene as it appeared to Frederick Philipse and his son Adolph.

In September 1956 my early test holes were aimed at three kinds of information: the ancient course of the Pocantico, the early docks, the original contour of the land beside the house, and seventeenth- and eighteenth-century foundations. In addition, I kept a daily tally of the tides, for here—as at Saugus—I was working in an area considerably altered by the rising sea level and the settling of land. Although the Pocantico is twenty-eight miles north of New York harbor, it lies in the course of the Hudson's tidal backwash. We had to keep pumps going continuously to be able to do any testing along the shoreline or in the river itself, and we could work there only when the tide was low.

The first fifty days of the survey indicated that the now filled-in Philipse harbor had been as large as several city blocks, and that the Pocantico had been much wider in the seventeenth century. About six feet deep in the riverside soils we found the first of the logs that were part of old docks, and in getting to this depth the men turned up the expected artifacts—fragments of clay pipes, handmade nails, earthenware, and shoe leather, as well as broken grindstones, pewter, silver, and colonial buttons. On this rested the decision to go ahead.

We are still digging at Philipsburg Manor as I write this. When all the evidence, both historical and archaeological, is finally gathered, a cohesive interpretation can be made. But in the meantime we can draw on more than two years during which the earth has been producing a continuing story of life beside the Pocantico River.

By the time we settled into the project the first week of January 1957, I had become friends with Robert Wheeler, the Sleepy

Hollow research director. Frequently as I crossed the footbridge in the thin early-morning light, I would hear myself hailed and there he would be, swinging along behind me. His interest in the preceding day's excavations was always intense, and often we found that sleep had led us to identical interpretations. Search of real-estate transactions by his staff sometimes showed references to structures which my diggers were uncovering. Sometimes his work pointed to the possible existence of a structure of which I was able to find no trace. Our separate discoveries were submitted to constant challenge and comparison in those morning meetings.

I was lucky, too, in finding in Herbie Bianchine a mechanical-equipment operator who can handle a back hoe with great skill. His hands are as gentle and sure as a pianist's as he manipulates the dozen levers that control the action of his steel-toothed scoop. One day Herbie said to me: "Boss, you must have X-ray eyes. How else could you see through this dirt and figure out the bottom of the old bay?"

"Herbie," I said, "without you, it would take fifty men to get rid of the fill soils covering up what we want to get at."

And it was true. After test pits and trenches had revealed the contours of the fills added by various occupants of the estate, the mechanical shovel removed the layers as efficiently as if we had been on our knees with spades and trowels.

Just as remarkable as Herbie's skill was the fact that so much evidence remained of changes made by the various owners of the Manor. American builders are inclined to scoop out all traces of old foundations before erecting a new building, and therefore archaeologists almost never have the opportunities afforded in the Old World, where as many as twelve levels have been stripped off a single site.

Compared to other rural American sites, the earth beside the Pocantico was unusual because the several owners had been so enthusiastic about building up the riverbank. The Saugus Iron-works had been abandoned and the site gradually reclaimed by nature, but the Philipse riveryard had been remodeled several times—one generation building on top of the structures of its predecessor. When shipping activity ceased, the riveryard was deliberately buried and the area was landscaped with lawns and gardens. This remodeling was made necessary by the natural settling of the land, the increase of the tidal plane and the silting that took place at the docks.

These factors made my work both more engrossing and more confusing. Although in the survey excavations we had found early docks, preserved by a water table, it was the meticulous digging during the following spring which brought to light a corduroy road—a road made by laying logs side by side. Buried in the mud, it started from the sloping ledgestone near the house and led in the direction of the present mill. Trenches dug here showed that a stone pier had been built on top of the road, and that parts of the pier, now deep in soggy soil, had been used in the foundation of the mill reproduction. Digging deeper proved that the stone pier had been laid in mud which had collected over the road. For forty days we pumped water out of this area. We unearthed a second dock extending from the stone pier, and at one of its corners I had Herbie sink a test hole seven feet deep. In the deep muds below the dock we found earthenware sherds, shoe leather, nails, clay pipes, and pieces of coral. It was clear that Nature had been busily filling up the Pocantico since the first dam had turned a quickly flowing stream into a sluggish one. There could have been no mud when the first settlers arrived, and therefore it was apparent that what we were finding was not of the earliest occupation.

As we dug below the second dock we found a second corduroy road. Pieces of a boat's hull as well as logs had gone into its con-struction. After carefully plotting the location and removing this evidence, we found several feet of mud below—an accumulation which was carefully sifted. Again we realized we had not reached the earliest level because this mud contained many relics associated with the Philipse trading era. Beneath the mud, resting only three or four inches above the peat bed of the old stream, we found collapsed sills of what may have been a log bridge joining

Logs used in construction of docks built in 1683 were found on top of natural peat and covered with tons of mud.

Log bridge that may have linked dock with shore collapsed and was buried where it fell. Behind workman can be seen partially excavated structure, made of logs laid side by side.

the ledge to the first dock. Following the bridge ruins into the stream led us to the log cribbing of the earliest dock.

Long before the mud had collected, Philipse's workmen had built this dock on natural peat at sufficient distance from the shore so that ample draft was provided for the anchored boats. The scarcity of silts and artifacts below this bridge indicated that it must have collapsed at an early date. Years later, when the upper dock was built upon this site, so much silt had collected that there no longer was any water between the ledgestone and the dock area.

In finding the original river bed we had determined that it was now covered with an eight-foot layer of mud that hadn't been there in the seventeenth century. Silt had begun the process of

The Philipse Dynasty

filling up the site after the first dam was erected, and men had helped by dumping refuse here, building new docks at higher levels as the river bed was raised. In this process the stream's course had changed, and finally the small bay the Dutch called *Die Schlappering Haven* had been eliminated. Day in, day out, year after year, the tide swept in past the stone house, slipped out to leave behind its sedimentary deposits. Had no dam been built, the quick stream would have washed its own course clean. But men had tampered with Nature, and Nature repaid them by burying docks and roadways in silt and mud.

Herbie trucked the mud that had covered the docking area to

Section showing stratifications and relics found at site of early mill and docks.

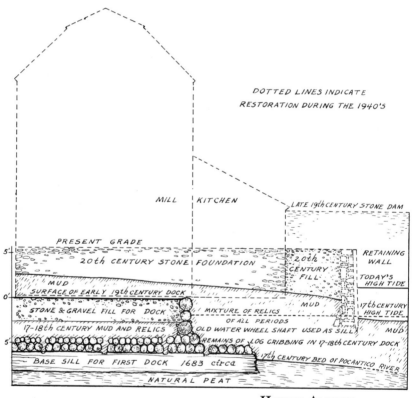

DOTTED LINES INDICATE
RESTORATION DURING THE 1940's

MILL KITCHEN

LATE 19th CENTURY STONE DAM

PRESENT GRADE

5' — 20th CENTURY STONE FOUNDATION — 20th CENTURY FILL — RETAINING WALL

MUD — TODAY'S HIGH TIDE

SURFACE OF EARLY 19th CENTURY DOCK

0' — STONE & GRAVEL FILL FOR DOCK — MIXTURE OF RELICS OF ALL PERIODS — MUD — 17th CENTURY HIGH TIDE

17-18th CENTURY MUD AND RELICS — OLD WATER WHEEL SHAFT USED AS SILL — MUD

5' — REMAINS OF LOG CRIBBING IN 17-18th CENTURY DOCK

17th CENTURY BED OF POCANTICO RIVER

BASE SILL FOR FIRST DOCK 1683 circa

NATURAL PEAT

HIDDEN AMERICA

My daughters, Jean and Bonnie Robbins, inspect the excavated docks while pumps keep the area free of water.

The Philipse Dynasty

DIG-IT-YOURSELF SOILS

are invited to help the
unearth the Dutch Trade
soils, removed from the dock

find nails, metals, earthenware
..ces, leather, yellow and red beads etc.
animal bones and are therefore from
..ings eaten by the early Dutch settlers.
..ease place your "FINDS" in our labeled
dy boxes.

Thank you for helping Us!

SIFTING TRAYS

Visitors to the project satisfy the urge to search for artifacts.

the periphery of the excavation. We labeled the mud pile "Dig-It-Yourself soils," and supplied garden tools to all visitors who wanted to try their hand at archaeology. Painstaking examination had removed every artifact that could increase our knowledge of the site, but scores of common items were left for visitors to turn up as they passed the earth through the sieves we had provided. As many as one hundred and fifty in a single day—adults as well as youngsters—have scrabbled here for hours with the help and guidance of my assistant. Their finds were added to the artifacts we had removed from these muds. The more interesting pieces made their way to our exhibit cases where the finder's name was displayed with his discovery.

No such liberty is possible at most archaeological projects, but I am convinced that this contact with the soil and with the tools of

HIDDEN AMERICA

archaeology demonstrated to hundreds of people the amount of buried historical evidence that remains.

Some of the proof of the world-wide importance of Philipse trading included the discovery here of clay pipes made in England, German salt-glaze dishes, Dutch pottery, Chinese porcelain, and coral from the West Indies. We found perforated shoe leather cut in the shapes of soles and heels, sleigh bells, an Adolph Philipse spoon, iron hinges, padlocks, gunflints, plates, an early work sled of oak and iron, knives, and brass jew's-harps which, sadly, were no longer melodic because they had lost their metal tongues during the centuries of burial.

The log construction runs to the northwest corner of the mill foundation, and our testing indicates similar wooden construction continuing beneath the stone walls. Now that the mill has been dismantled, there are many future possibilities. Meanwhile, we have a fairly clear picture of the earliest dock. It was formed of boulders and hard-packed soil, framed by logs projecting from the river

Pit dug by mechanical shovel cut into underground water table and revealed one of large logs used in dock construction.

bank. A free log, floating with the changes of the tide, was attached to the dock only by chains or ropes. Sloops of about forty feet in length could be tied up to the floating log rather than to the dock itself. When the tide was in, even an ocean-going brig could stand by while cargo was transferred to a warehouse, or while ground corn or other produce from the manor was loaded. In the construction of the upper dock, we found an intriguing feature: a shaft of a large water wheel had been put to use in building the base sill. That part of a wheel should have been available for such use seemed to indicate that a water-powered mill, more ancient than the dock, had been dismantled. It seems unlikely that such a piece of wood would have been transported any distance at a time when the land was covered with forests.

There is no question that Frederick Philipse operated at least

Fragment of wine bottle found at Philipsburg Manor with initials of Adolph Philipse. A spoon found here bears the same monogram.

one mill, and the continuing excavations may lead us to more exact knowledge of his operations. Small artifacts—in one area only twenty-five feet square we found a cache of more than 13,000—are now undergoing intensive study by specialists.

Artisanship has always been necessary in the establishment of any small community, and evidences of the making of lime, bricks, and other building materials are prime targets in our current digging. We are equally interested in the man-made changes in the contours of the mill pond. Test pits reaching the original pond bottom prove conclusively that the northerly shoreline was filled and pushed southward more than forty feet. The evidence removed from below this fill shows that the change took place just after the cessation of the Philipse reign.

It was in this area that I discovered how treacherous is man's technique of depositing soil as compared with the solid packing done by Nature. Some thirty-five feet from the pond I had indicated a spot where I wanted Herbie to dig with the back hoe, going down the full eleven-foot reach of his machine. Previous tests had shown that this area had been filled, and I wanted now to check the artifacts at this point against those of other holes. When Herbie had slit a trench two feet wide, ten feet long, and eleven feet deep, one of the shovel men, named Joe, came to find me.

"Mister Robbie," he said in his thick Czech accent, "we hit bottom."

I climbed down a ladder to inspect the condition of the filled-in pond surface and to have a look at any relics there might be.

Sure enough, the sand toward the bottom of the ladder was oozing with water. Herbie's blade had cut into the sub-soil, so I bent over to measure the thickness of the silt that had collected before the fill-in. Very carefully I shaved through the mud in

The Philipse Dynasty

search of artifacts. I saw a glint of white and reached to pick up the bowl of a clay pipe.

"*Boss!*"

High above my head I heard Herbie's voice, and behind me the unmistakable sound of earth on the move. Automatically, I started toward the ladder.

It was too late. Damp sand rushed in around me. I was caught with one foot raised, like some of those who tried to escape the lava of Vesuvius. I flailed my arms and somehow managed to keep them free as the sand encased me up to my shoulders.

Water oozed into my boots, tugging downward. I could think of nothing but wet cement. I felt the effect of tremendous pressure being applied to every square centimeter of my submerged body. I tried to force my raised leg downward, but it would not budge. I strained to put all my strength into the toes of my other leg, hoping to find a foundation, a purchase by which to push myself upward. But there was nothing solid, nothing but pressure. The weight pushed at my rib cage, as if to force the last air out of my lungs.

With no time to think, I felt the sudden movement of the sand as Joe and his partner John came to the edge of the hole, shouting curses and swinging their shovels frantically. They stamped above me as the sand sifted down from their feet.

"Get away!" I shouted. I knew that one big foot was all that was necessary to start a small avalanche that would cover me completely. "Get back from the edge!"

I could hear Herbie pleading with them.

"Mister Robbie—" Joe's bull-strong body was trembling with indecision.

"Get!" I coughed. I felt the rage within me as the grip of dislodged earth encircled my chest. I shouted again, "Move!" and added a few well-chosen words.

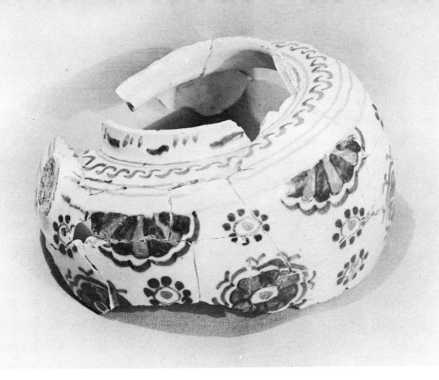

Pieces found scattered in the ground at Philipsburg Manor were sorted, then fitted together to form part of a polychrome jar.

Frantic as they were to help, John and Joe were doing nothing but making the cave-in more treacherous.

"Get back, will you?" I said. "You're too heavy."

At the top, calmer than I, Herbie persuaded my pachydermic helpers to leave the edge of the pit and to stand by to haul up sand. Then he eased himself lithely down, and used a shovel to lift the pressure away from my torso. By the time my knees were exposed, my legs were so numb I didn't seem able to move them and Herbie pulled me up like a tight cork from a bottle.

"How you feel, Mister Robbie?" Joe asked.

I was chagrined. If I hadn't been in such a hurry I would have paid more attention to the condition of the pit walls before I went in.

The happier result of that pit, combined with others in which

The Philipse Dynasty

I was more careful, is that we have now plotted the pond's perimeter, just as it was in the seventeenth century, on the master grid on which every change in the Philipse acres is being recorded. When this work is finished, there will be an archaeological account of all the phases of construction that have left vestiges during almost three centuries of white occupation. The greatest satisfaction may lie in fully-detailed knowledge of the nineteen years of the first Frederick Philipse's ownership, simply because it goes furthest back in antiquity. But archaeology is less than totally effective when the knowledge it produces is self-contained. We need to know the influences passed on from one era to another; and as we start backwards from the twentieth century it is important to develop a record of the evolution which links today with the earliest period of habitation.

I have mentioned that we found one foundation site which had served five occupations. It occupies the most logical location for the first warehouse—on the sloping ledgestone within easy carting distance of the collapsed log bridge. Although the excavation at this spot is not finished, we found in removing the fill from the ledge that the stone had been cut back and leveled off to accommodate a structure roughly twice the size of the twentieth century utilities building which now stands here. Digging around the present building revealed that it had been erected on the foundations of a late nineteenth or early twentieth century dwelling, and digging deeper showed us the thick stone walls of an earlier ice house. Before 1850, there had been an outdoor oven here. If the first structure was indeed a warehouse, that would account for the cutting down of the ledge to the level of the log bridge close by.

To visit Philipsburg Manor today is to see it in upheaval. No longer does a green lawn reach from the stone house to surround the mill and end neatly at a wall beside the water. The earth has opened up. Now the terrain drops naturally away from the house, as it did when Frederick Philipse first sailed through *Die Schlappering Haven* to find the shore upon which to build his dock. And the dock is there—still wallowing in the sediment of centuries. As we dig farther and farther, removing more and more evidence of nineteenth- and twentieth-century living, we seem to see another world rising from the depths: the world of the Hudson Valley as it once was. With continued diligence, our digging beside the old stone house will help tell a more detailed story of the Dutch in America than has been told before.

6

The Vikings: Vinland Revisited

ARCHAEOLOGISTS ARE like detectives. We have to reconstruct the drama with the scantiest of tangible evidence. We have to develop theories and attempt to arrive at brilliant deductions. Sometimes, like fictional sleuths in mystery novels, we go too far in our theorizing—yet no archaeologist would be worth his salt if he were totally without imagination. I don't know which is worse—an archaeologist so imaginative he fails to hold himself in check or one so literal he fails to interpret his material adequately.

Archaeology needs, frequently, the techniques of the natural and social sciences. It needs the help of history whenever such help is available. It is, after all, a business of putting pieces together. In reconstructing an aspect of a culture, an archaeologist, according to one distinguished scholar, "can utilize the reconstruction that has been made by others, amplifying or correcting the previous point of view. His end is not to create beauty but to make us understand the reality that has disappeared."

Even a tangible discovery can sometimes mislead the archaeologist. The find in such cases becomes the source of great controversy, sometimes continuing for decades. Battle lines are drawn and each side does its best to convince the other.

Such a controversy still rages over the saga of the vikings in America. It is a controversy in which I found myself invited to take part shortly after I had found the water wheel under Central Street. The question was: Did Leif Ericsson, or members of his party, leave clues on Cape Cod that might prove fruitful to archaeologists?

There have been at least forty-six theories about the location of the area which the vikings called Vinland. It has been placed in Nova Scotia, Maine, Rhode Island, at the mouth of the Hudson River, and in New Jersey. In the last hundred years nine interpreters had staked a viking claim on Cape Cod, but no one had made so valiant a defense of that claim as did Frederick J. Pohl who, after eighteen years of hot pursuit, singled out the south shore of Follins Pond, near the present town of North Dennis.

Carrying his theory like a banner, this retired Brooklyn school teacher visited Cape Cod for the first time in 1947. Along the shore of Mill Pond, Follins Pond, and the Bass River he quickly located a series of holes drilled into a group of boulders which to his mind were incontrovertibly the mooring holes used by Ericsson's men during the winter they spent in Vinland.

The publication in 1951 of Pohl's reconstruction of the viking saga crackled like lightning. Skeptics howled, and romantics gloried in the "proof." Letters from many people, including Pohl, flooded the office of the Massachusetts Archaeological Society. At every meeting we found ourselves involved in pro and con discussions, and soon it was clear that—unendowed though the

The Vikings: Vinland Revisited

Society was—the members would have to subject the new theory to an archaeological test. A volunteer dig was organized under the leadership of Benjamin L. Smith, chairman of the research council.

What made Frederick Pohl so convincing in his belief that excavation would support his carefully nurtured ideas?

He had immersed himself in viking lore. Meticulously he had traced the saga in the ancient *Hauksbok* and the *Flateyjarbok*, the two accounts of the viking voyages written in Old Norse. Like a talented detective, he had piled up clue upon clue, studying the references to flora and fauna, studying geological observations, collating the geographical references until all the signs pointed in what he was sure was one direction only.

The *Flateyjarbok* told of a voyage to a shore Pohl identified as Newfoundland, then on to Nova Scotia. One day, the saga relates, the Ericsson fleet "sailed from thence over the open ocean with a northeast wind, and were out two days before they saw land. Approaching this land, they came upon an island which lay to the north of the land. They went ashore upon this island and looked about them. It proved a fine day, and they found dew upon the grass . . . Back on the ship, they sailed into a sound between the island and that cape which went to the north from the land, and steered to the west of the cape. It was very shallow there at ebb tide and they ran aground, and it was a long distance to look from the ship to the sea. They were so curious to go ashore that they could not wait until the tide rose, but hastened to the land, where a river flowed down from a lake. As soon as the tide floated their ship, however, they rowed in the boat back to the ship, which they steered up the river and into the lake where they anchored. They carried their gear ashore and built themselves temporary shelters."

Analyzing this busy day in the year 1003, Pohl spent hours in the map room of the public library. What was the island the vikings came upon "north of the land"? One night he woke with a start. In a dream he had seen the island of Nantucket. Jutting out from the north shore of Nantucket was a slim spit of sand at the end of which was a rise of ground called Great Point. In Pohl's dream, high tide covered the spit and made Great Point an island. Nantucket, he reasoned, was large enough to have been mistaken by the vikings for "land." The island north of the land had to be Great Point; it was the only one to fit the saga's descriptions. He got out of bed and studied his maps. There, across from Great Point, was the south shore of Cape Cod. There a river flowed down from a lake. Pohl convinced himself that Leif Ericsson and his men had entered the mouth of the Bass River, rowing inland for about six miles before camping on the shore of Follins Pond. "I knew," he said later in a report to the Massachusetts Archaeological Society, "that it was the invariable custom of the early Norse to haul up a ship on shore for the winter, and to build a shed over it for its protection."

In August 1947, on his first trip to Dennis, Pohl rowed across the lake, and as he approached the southerly shore, he noted that the wind grew gentler, indicating to him that this side of the lake would have offered the best shelter a thousand years before. Five hundred yards from shore he spotted a skerry between his boat and the beach. The giant boulder jutted nine feet out of the water. On the shoreward rim of the skerry, he assured himself, there must be a hole in which an iron stake could be lodged to hold a ship's line. He was right. Slanting into the crest of the stone was an inch-wide slot, obviously made by man, and in Pohl's mind the man who made it could have been none other than a viking. After several more years of research, and the publication of his findings, he brought his theory to our archaeological society.

He told Howard C. Mandell, then the society's president, that he wanted us to dig for evidence of a ship that had been shored. On Follins Pond he had picked out a site—a gully near the skerry which to him seemed the most logical spot for the Norse to beach their ship. Here he found a tiny strand about 35 feet wide, slanting upward about five feet in its total length of 160 feet. Hills rise between 25 and 35 feet one each side of the gully, and elsewhere along the pond's south shore are large boulders and a steep bank that varies from 25 to 70 feet in height. If the vikings had left behind them any clues that could survive almost a thousand years, this might well be the place to find them.

"How big a ship?" Howard Mandell asked Pohl.

"About 65 feet over-all length with an 18 foot beam."

Pohl had in mind an ocean-going viking ship with a level keel for most of her length, a curved dragon's head on her high, narrow prow, and a stern of equal height—a one-master with a single square sail raised by a windlass, without decks but with space amidships for cargo, and thwarts for rowers near the ends. "She was double-ended," he said, "with graceful lines." But his picture seemed improbable on a pond only three-quarters of a mile long.

Pohl conferred with Ben Smith, who by this time had lined up his volunteer diggers in groups, one of which I was asked to direct. On the basis of Pohl's reasoning, coupled with a reconnaissance of the terrain made by Ross Moffett, it was determined that there were five highly suspect areas strung out along the edge of the pond. When digging got under way on a Saturday in May 1952, there were fifty persons equipped with shovels. Most of them were amateur members of the society, but a few non-members who had written convincing letters were also signed on. Those in my group were assigned to the high table land west of the gully. Although a grid pattern was laid out and we dug two hundred test pits in this area, only one produced any evidence whatever of early occupation. At this spot we were led to a shallow, saucer-shaped

Indian fireplace paved with fist-sized cobblestones and filled with charcoal and oyster shells. Thorough investigation that day failed to bring to light either tools or other artifacts.

My own doubt as to the probability of the Pohl theory had, for the moment, been justified—at least in the area in which my crew had been digging. But there was still that gulley, the focal point of all of Frederick Pohl's hopes. I was very curious, as we abandoned the field after the first day's work, to learn what luck had fallen to the diggers under my friend, Maurice Robbins.

At the Lincoln Lodge in Harwichport, where the group leaders met that evening with Mr. Pohl, the seismic rumble of controversy got under way immediately. The author of the Follins Pond theory could scarcely contain himself. He was sure that the Maurice Robbins group, digging in the gully, had struck pay dirt. In less than twenty minutes after their spades had cut into the turf, a vertical post three inches in diameter had been exposed. The fact that this was along the median line of the gully was extremely significant to Pohl. Excavation revealed the remains of a two-foot-long red cedar stake buried thirteen inches underground. Its lower end had been sharpened to facilitate driving and it rested on a flat stone with two smaller stones buttressing it. Obviously, as Pohl pointed out, it had been set to bear a weight. Was it a keel-bearing? A shipways built by a viking crew?

Maurice Robbins told us that, using the stake they had found and a heavy beam adjacent to it as a base, he had sketched the possible form of a primitive shoring. When his crew had dug trenches where his sketch indicated additional props might exist, they found ten more posts. Five of these made a sort of center line; they were all reinforced with stones and, except for one with a point, seemed to have been set in excavated holes. Six smaller pointed stakes indicated the approximate outline of a boat or ship. "If we suppose that this is indeed the remains of a cradle or sup-

Digging by members of the Massachusetts Archaeological Society revealed ship's shoring outline convenient to water.

port for a beached boat of some sort," Maurice Robbins said, "the length of the craft is suggested to have been about 70 feet, the rise of the bow nearly four feet and the width something over 16 feet."

Frederick Pohl smiled in satisfaction. The measurements were almost identical with those he had given Howard Mandell.

Yet the atmosphere of the meeting in the Lodge was charged with questions from those who had not been present and wanted to be sure. Maurice Robbins reviewed the day's activity. He said that preliminary examination showed that the floor of the gully at its midpoint is about three feet above mean highwater and that, except for a small area, it had never been disturbed by man. There was a growth of grasses with some small brush, and several trees which had to be felled. Three trenches had been laid out and subsequently interconnected. "The appearance of the profiles," he said, "suggests that this area once supported a growth of red cedar and that later this forest growth was succeeded by swampy plants growing under very wet conditions, possibly caused by water flowing from springs in the northern slope, or from flooding at high water periods from the pond itself. The presence of a cedar log some 58 inches below the present surface bears out this hypothesis."

But to my mind it was not a hypothesis which proved that Leif the Lucky had ever sailed in Follins Pond. The age of the wood of the stakes had yet to be determined, and my study of tides at Saugus had helped to establish that there had been at least a three-foot submergence in the New England coastline since 1650. This meant that the floor of the gully at the point where the stakes were found would have been too elevated three centuries ago to have been reached by a boat at high tide—undoubtedly it had been a great deal higher in the days of the viking voyages.

Since that weekend, experts have gathered considerable data to establish the varying position of the sea during the past 20,000 years. Carbon 14 tests of ice age shell deposits in the Chesapeake Bay area, for instance, have showed that the Atlantic is fifteen to fifty feet higher today than it was 4,000 to 7,000 years ago— indicating that during that prehistoric period there either was no Chesapeake Bay at all or that the area contained so little water that it could not be compared to the bay as we know it today. A similar change has taken place at Cape Cod. With the level of the

The Vikings: Vinland Revisited

sea rising slowly but continuously, and the land settling at about ten inches a century, it can be assumed that even a thousand years ago Follins Pond was no wetter than a swamp and the Bass River was only a brook. Much of what was then the shoreline of Cape Cod is now covered by the rising waters of the Atlantic and Massachusetts Bay.

Unfortunately we did not have the results of these carbon-dating studies in 1952, and our meeting in the Lincoln Lodge broke up with unanswered questions in the minds of most of us. We gathered the following morning in a mood to track down the last clue that might help to support the Pohl theory. Light showers during the night, a glowering sky and a promise of further rain cut the ranks of diggers, but my group worked that morning to exhaust the site where we had found the Indian fireplace. There was not a sign of Norse occupation. Ross Moffett's team excavated a site—at which Pohl saw the possiblility of graves—and found no bones or artifacts. Meanwhile, Dr. Henry F. Howe and Donn Haglund spent the morning mapping the location of the holes drilled in boulders which might have been chiseled by the Vikings to moor their craft. They found and examined seven more than Frederick Pohl had found and concluded they had been made for blasting purposes. Why such holes in rocks that had not been blasted? It is a matter of record that in 1898, when the mile-and-a-half long Bass River Breakwater was built, every movable large stone in the area was carried by team, drag, sledge, and scow to the site. When the builders ran out of portable rocks they blasted big ones. To do this, they first drilled a hole very much like the ones the vikings are known to have made on the rocky, treeless Scandinavian fiords where mooring is a problem. In such holes the blasters placed charges of dynamite to shatter the giants into sizes that could be handled. They stopped blasting when enough rock had been moved to fill the breakwater.

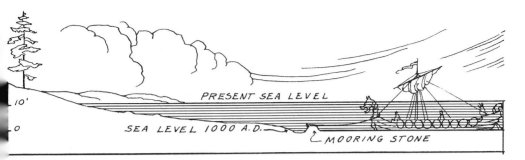

PRESENT SEA LEVEL

SEA LEVEL 1000 A.D.

MOORING STONE

10'

0

The shoreline of viking times has been inundated by changes in sea level.

Yet even though Pohl's interest in the mooring holes had been thus well dampened, our expedition still had to contend with a buried structure which was quite apparently a ship's shoring of some past era. When I joined the diggers who had exposed this site, I was immediately curious about their principal trench. Still *in situ* was a stake seventeen inches long with a sharply pointed end which had been driven down until it struck a large rock buried there by a glacier, not by the hand of man. Five inches of the lowest part of the stake was embedded in damp peat and the next three inches in a mixture of peat and sand, also damp. But the upper nine inches of this well-preserved wood had been above the water table in a sandy soil which had been alternately wet and dry. Wood is destroyed by bacteria which require oxygen to live. Where the oxygen in the air is permanently sealed off by water, wood will retain its form for centuries. But when earth dries out, or when its condition fluctuates between wet and dry, wood will rot away in a few years.

There was no chance that the stakes unearthed could have lasted as long as a hundred years. In addition, I found here, twenty-seven inches beneath the surface, a wire nail of the type not manufactured until the 1880's, and twelve inches down I

The Vikings: Vinland Revisited

turned up a coal briquet. Other diggers found an adze, and other more or less contemporary artifacts. Though they were not associated with the stakes, they were too close to them to lend credence to the thousand-year-old theory. It became the conclusion of the leaders of the dig which Frederick Pohl had initiated that the shoring was probably not more than one hundred years old and that the vikings had had no need to chisel holes for mooring along a river on which trees grew to the water's edge, where ships could have been anchored at the stern and tied by a bowline to a tree.

"We have neither proved nor disproved Mr. Pohl's theories," Ben Smith told the members of the Massachusetts Archaeological Society after we had decamped from Cape Cod. "He may be entirely correct, but nothing in our two days of intensive investigation of the area indicates that the viking settlement of Vinland was located on Follins Pond."

Frederick Pohl still feels strongly that his theory is the best of all those concerning the Ericsson exploration of America. As the result of our Cape Cod findings he made a study of U.S. shipbuilding. In the Massachusetts Archaeological Bulletin some three years after our dig, he wrote: "The absolute conclusion can be drawn that every known type of American ship, of the size indicated, was two or three times too heavy to have been supported on the keel-bearing posts and stones in the Follins Pond gully." Was there ever a vessel light enough? "There was one such type, and so far as is known, only one," his report says. "A vessel of the ancient Norse type, of lap-streak or clinker-built construction, of 69' over-all and 18' beam, would weigh, without her equipment, 10 to 13 tons. The 9th century Gokstad ship in the Oslo Museum, 76½" over-all, 17' beam, equipped weighed (according to Professor A. W. Brogger's estimate in *The Viking Ships*) 20.2 metric tons, about 22½ short tons. Stripped, it weighed less than 15 tons.

Open Viking ships were thus lightly built to give them wave-riding qualities. One feature of the clinker-built ships was that they lacked rigidity and were actually flexible.

"A vessel of the viking type of trading ship," he went on, "stripped, would be easily hauled up with very simple gear by thirty men, and blocking to preserve her shape would be of the simplest kind. The keel-bearing posts and stones in the Follins Pond gully were set up for a ship that weighed as little as a Viking ship. Since no other type of ship in all the history of shipbuilding could have been supported on the shoring, the shoring appears to be evidence of ancient Norse occupancy of the south shore of Follins Pond. It eloquently calls for further archaeological investigation."

Certainly the as yet unestablished probability that Norse sailors came to America deserves further investigation, and it is my conviction that digs like our Follins Pond excursion are worth the time and manpower involved. Yet I'm convinced that any stone containing a mooring hole which one might find today along a shoreline was too high above the water a thousand years ago to have served any seaworthy purpose. With the ocean rising at the rate of a foot a century, today's shoreline would have been high and dry in the era of Leif the Lucky. Wherever the vikings sailed, it was certainly not in Follins Pond.

As recently as the early part of 1959 there was a new discovery on Cape Cod that some enthusiasts hoped might furnish the long-sought proof that Norsemen had really been here. Near Bourne, on Buzzards Bay, a man digging peat accidentally exposed a sizable wood fragment which he judged to have been the top rib section of a boat. The first excited inspection linked the fragment to similarly shaped pieces in viking ships, but as this is written no expert has been convinced.

Yet the viking cause still has a devoted champion in Frederick

Pohl. He has spent a quarter century at it. He has studied the saga descriptions of Vinland so well that he is sure that some day he will be able to apply them to the New England we know today. His is the kind of dedication that archaeology needs. But archaeology also needs the kind of scientific examination of evidence which we applied at Follins Pond.

7

Who Discovered America?

WHO DISCOVERED AMERICA? I'm sure of this: it wasn't Columbus. I'm also sure that it will be a long time before we can settle on the one true answer. For there are too many unsolved riddles, too many clues which have been destroyed by negligence or vandalism.

Of the existing clues there are too many that are so problematical they may never be accurately interpreted. Like Frederick Pohl's Project Vinland, the theories are often sound enough, but excavations fail to produce the clinching argument. The stone beehive-like structures of New England have stirred the fancies of theoreticians for generations, and any boy growing up in Massachusetts as I did could hardly escape the notions about them. Yet it was not until I was deep in the dig at Saugus that I realized how anxious others were to have them explained. Repeatedly, visitors to the Ironworks urged me to investigate strange structures in their communities. By far the one most often mentioned was the stone "village" at North Salem, New Hampshire, seen by some as the druidic stonehenge of America, believed by others to be a shrine built by Irish missionaries in the ninth century, eyed cynically by others as the work of an eccentric.

It was not the possibility of a clinching argument that moved me to drive to North Salem in 1953, but my own curiosity, whetted by the many unanswered questions. The most exploited theory, put forth by a sincere archaeological amateur named William B. Goodwin, was that the stone ruins at Cowbell Corners had once been the central point in a network of stone structures erected by Irish monks of the Culdee order after they had been driven westward from Iceland in about A. D. 874.

Goodwin had found in the sagas of the Norsemen the story of Bjarni Heriulfsson who, 492 years before Columbus, had gone from Iceland to the coast of America "in the vicinity of Great Ireland where the people spoke Irish and had Irish names." These Irish-speaking people (Goodwin said) were first noted on the Greenland expedition of Thorfinn Karlsefni, an explorer who had married the widow of Leif Ericsson's brother. Goodwin was sure of "remarkable proof" that in the environs of Vinland Karlsefni had run into Irish Culdee monks who, the sagas asserted, "wear white robes, bear banners on poles and march in procession, shouting loudly."

Goodwin cited "the definite report that had come back to Iceland, that at the same time Bjarni had sailed from Iceland in 1000, Ari Marson, another Icelander, had been driven westward to America, had there been seized and forcibly baptized and compelled to remain with his captors in Great Ireland." Karlsefni came along early in the eleventh century and fortuitously bumped into three men who had been captured with Ari Marson, who told of the "white robed men who dwelled in caves and dens." Here was easy evidence that, even before the Vikings, Europeans had found the sea route to America. The Culdees, whose name derives from the Latin for "God's comrade," were hermit priests whom Goodwin believed had settled in New England after various escapes from plundering Norsemen. From aboriginal granite each man had built his private cell. And on the high ground above the Spicket River Goodwin saw them erecting a complement of edifices which was their Vatican.

This North Salem site as it exists today has been described as a cluster of stone huts, houses, shelters and altars, walls and wells, ramps and drains, guard-houses and streets, a plaza, and a Y-shaped structure some have thought to be the ruins of a church building. The story goes that the hermit monks gathered here when their bishop called them from their missionary posts among the Indians. There is even a giant slab with a deep rectangular drainage groove which has become known as the "sacrificial stone"—the indelicate suggestion being that these early Christian travelers still clung to pagan habits. It lies eerily in the dappling shadow of young white birches and pines, convenient to the cross-marked altar and the slab-topped huts so low that any average-sized human would have to crawl in. Goodwin thought it more likely that the grooved stone had been used by the Culdees as a wine press, and there is another theory that the monks scrubbed their white robes here, letting the dirty water drain away in the chiseled channel.

As I walked up the hill to the man-made caves on a bright November afternoon, I was immediately aware of what at first glance seemed to be a typical New England stone wall to my left. An unusual quality caught my eye: the wall incorporated large stone lintels in the construction, sometimes crowning window-like openings. The laying of the lintels was remarkably like the work

Who Discovered America?

135

of the cave builders. Yet I was sure that Irish monks would have had no need for this kind of stone fence so important to early Yankee farmers. Through my mind flashed the thought of Seth Jonathan Pattee who from 1826 to 1848 had owned the farm on which this site was found. I had heard many stories about him, and I could see him as an eccentric gifted with a fine imagination—making himself out to be the reincarnation of some ancient, primitive cliff dweller, monk, king, or what have you. Yet the structures were too intriguing to be dismissed so cursorily.

That afternoon I dug a test trench and turned up pottery sherds and bits of charcoal; three or four inches under the base stones of a wall I found the remains of a nail resting on the natural, fine sand subsoil. These post-Revolutionary artifacts were suspiciously close to the caves.

On my second day at the site I studied the great Y-shaped cavern. A giant boulder which may weigh as much as 70 tons forms the easterly wall of a passageway leading to a fireplace. In the whole complement of structures there are many other large stones, some weighing ten, some twenty, thirty, or forty tons. Had these been tugged into place—like the monuments at Stonehenge —by men who had neither machinery nor draft animals? It didn't seem likely. All the structures are formed entirely of native laminated stone and set upon the solid bedrock of the hill, which was worn smooth on its southern exposure by glacial action. There are literally thousands of stones, either still in place in existing walls or scattered about in rubble. This group of buildings was erected 275 feet above sea level, forty-odd miles from the New Hampshire coast and almost equally distant from the Merrimack River. It is the work of an engineer possessing an analytical mind. A drainage system had been skillfully constructed of stone slabs to keep the caverns dry.

On the basis of this early investigation I decided to devote my

Grooved stone on North Salem, New Hampshire, farm that legend says was carved for human sacrifices.

next busman's holiday to a site I had stumbled across in walks with my children twelve years earlier. Less than 200 yards from my home in Lincoln is a stone structure which would strike the casual eye as being just as mysterious as the North Salem buildings. Though it is just off a well-traveled highway, it has received little serious interest and had never been excavated before my Thanksgiving Day dig in 1953. Goodwin apparently had never heard of it because it is not included in his list of seventeen beehives which his theory relates to the discovery of America by the Irish.

Another North Salem stone bears chiseled "running deer" which may have been inspired by carved animal figures found in northern Europe.

Several visits here did little to lift the veil of mystery. Digging at various times with my wife, my son and daughters, and several willing friends, I found no sign of either artifacts or human burials. The main structure is roughly ten feet square and five feet high, put together of massive stones. It lies half hidden among young trees and brush, and at first glance resembles a pile of rubble. In the center of the roof, however, there is a crude, two-foot-wide circular entrance to a round room five feet in diameter. In this interior I dug out the debris and found a floor made of layers of stones to facilitate drainage. In one wall of the room was a ten-inch channel which proved to lead to a rectangular chamber now open to the sky. A narrow cobbled pavement led from this second chamber along the massive east wall of the main structure. At the point at which this pavement ends there was a roughly rectangular compartment set into the east wall. Not a trace of smoke or charcoal was to be found here, making it almost certain that the structure was not designed for any sort of outdoor oven. In fact, my work at this site turned up no sign of fire, inside or out. Examination of the surrounding terrain showed a ridge just west of the structure evidently made by soil excavated in leveling the base and floor. About forty feet to the east I noticed a similar ridge and, close to it, a settling of soil—the kind of depression in the earth which is almost a certain sign of an area that has been disturbed by man. I began to dig and, sure enough, I found another structure, this one so ruined that I couldn't determine its full dimensions.

Though I found nothing conclusive in these digs so close to my home, the Goodwin theory had so intrigued me that I was impelled to investigate some of the other beehives which he maintained had once been occupied by the Culdee hermits. I didn't expect them to be as regular in design, as reminiscent of real beehives—or igloos—as the stone shelters, built by monks during the

Entrance to underground structure at Upton, Massachusetts.

Dark Ages, which still survive in Ireland and Scotland. But many specialists had pointed out likenesses of technique between the dome-shaped architecture attributed to ancient Celts and the dry-laid stone structures found half-buried in New England towns and countryside.

Among the more controversial of these so-called beehives is one at Upton, Massachusetts, a structure so large that many visitors imagined that it had been used as a Culdee chapel. Certainly it fires the imagination. The legend surrounding it had gained so much stature that in 1954 the Massachusetts group known as the Trustees of Public Reservations were considering purchasing the property on which it is buried. Lawrence Fletcher, a member of that group, contacted me when I was restoring the site of the Dover Iron Works, near Boston, and I drove down to meet him in

Who Discovered America?

139

Upton one Friday morning in May. Sidney L. Beals and Albert Sherman, two other antiquarians, joined us, and the Boston Globe sent out two men. It was a gathering which I thought had been carefully arranged, but I found myself almost immediately the object of a tongue lashing.

Malcolm Pearson—who owned the site of the North Salem caves and was the son of the owner of the Upton structure—arrived and immediately challenged Lawrence Fletcher's intentions and my qualifications. Obviously agitated, he gave us the impression that he thought we were publicity seekers making use of his father's sacred beehive for some nefarious purpose. Only after Fletcher managed to explain that I had spent five years excavating at Saugus did he calm down. Yet he remained adamant in forbidding me to dig.

His glance took in my probe rods and he said: "None of those, either."

"Well, I can't do much testing without my rods," I said.

"Rods lead to shovels," he said bluntly.

So to make him happy, I put the rods away and took out the metal detector I had brought with me. Somewhat reluctantly Pearson extended a light on a long cord from the near-by Pearson house and led us to a low stone passage, about 120 feet from the house, which leads into the main chamber. We put on rubber boots and crouched down to make our way through the tunnel. Seepage had left three to four inches of water in the cavern and as the light flashed over the walls my eye was caught by a lintel stone directly opposite the entrance under which there was an obviously patched section; it was apparent that here had once been another entrance that now was stoned up. The cavern is spacious enough to accommodate a dozen people and it has a vaulted ceiling ten to twelve feet high. But no evidence suggested that excavation would do more than confirm the probability that it had been put together of local field stone simply to serve as a storage cellar. I noticed that its open entrance was incorporated into a stone fence, making it obvious that both structures had been built at the same time—almost certainly in either the eighteenth or nineteenth century. The cavern resembled a good many others I was to investigate in tracking down the legends of pre-Columbian occupation of New England.

I went on another expedition in 1954, this time to Elephant Hill Valley in the center of the Green Mountains. Here Goodwin reported that he had found a Culdee beehive located more than a mile from any other sign of habitation. By this time I'd seen enough of the structures to feel strongly that they represented nothing more mysterious than early Yankee artisanship, yet if this cave proved to be as remote as Goodwin maintained, an entirely new light would be thrown on the problem. With the editor of *Vermont Life* magazine and one of his staff members, I stopped in South Royalton and picked up Wendell Eaton, a life-long resident

Metal detector in hand, I inspect a large lintel in the interior wall of Upton "beehive" with Malcolm Pearson.

who had guided Goodwin to the site the latter had described as being so isolated. Some distance out of the village, turning off the narrow, climbing road, we left the station wagon and trudged up-hill to a sloping field where a small growth of young trees shaded a cavern entrance crowned by a great granite lintel. My eye was immediately caught by a stone wall leading to the beehive. Exactly as at Upton, the wall was incorporated into the entrance stones and then ran a few feet farther before branching off in another direction.

Wendell Eaton, a lean and typical Vermonter, turned to me and said: "Let's go into it."

"Not yet," I said. "First let me take a look at the surroundings." I walked about forty feet away from the entrance where I had spotted a leveled area and began poking the turf with my probe rod. At once I struck the foundation stones of a building, and I cleared away the overburden of brush and soil to show that in this instance Goodwin was certainly mistaken in believing the underground cave was remote from other evidence of habitation. At that site, excavation turned up the chimney of a house, the foundations of a barn, and the spring which had provided water for early farmers.

"Now," I said, "let's look at the beehive." It proved to be constructed in the same manner as the others I had inspected. We spent most of that hot August day looking into the several other structures which Wendell Eaton had pointed out to Goodwin. Not one of them was in any sense removed from civilization. They had been built, I felt sure, by pioneer Vermonters, as root cellars. To demonstrate my contention, I went back to the village hardware store and went through a pile of thermometers until I found two which registered identically. Back at the site, I put one in the cavern and one in the shade twenty-five feet outside the entrance. In the subterranean interior the mercury registered 55.5 degrees;

above ground the second thermometer showed 90. Clearly, no white-robed monk would choose to hibernate under such chilling conditions.

Professional obligations have left me no time to pursue the mystery of the New England beehives to the end, but some day I hope to study the problem closely. Meanwhile, there are others who are probing in this area. Archaeology proceeds step by step, with cumulative results. Each man's work contributes to the clearing away of the haze of obscurity. While I was digging at Jefferson's birthplace, for instance, an excavator at North Salem came to the conclusion that the eerie "village" had been built "certainly not prior to 1780 and in all probability . . . between 1826 and 1848," the years during which the property was farmed by Seth Jonathan Pattee.

Under the sponsorship of the Early Sites Foundation, Gary Vescelius of Yale University in six weeks of digging had turned up hundreds of the kind of artifacts I'd found in my hasty search under one of the walls. Vescelius's expedition came to the conclusion that although the caves might be compared to some European megalithic ruins, there was not enough similarity to accept a historical relationship. The Pattee family is said to have come from Brittany and the Jersey islands where ancient megalithic structures abound—making it easily conceivable that the eccentric Jonathan might have built the structures with this family heritage in the back of his mind.

A rotten white pine stump still rooted on top of one of the caves had long been cited as evidence that the strange buildings must have been erected before Jonathan Pattee's day. Examination indicated that it had taken root no later than 1800, which would force the conclusion that this single structure had been built by someone other than Jonathan—for in that year he was four years old. Yet Vescelius was convinced that there is every likelihood that

Who Discovered America?

143

Pattee's father or his grandfather was responsible for the beginning of Jonathan's weird housing development.

The most crushing blow to the defenders of the Culdee theory was the evidence that the Y-shaped cavern, most important of the buildings, is less than two centuries old. Vescelius's digging also suggested to him that the Y cavern, which abuts the "sacrificial" stone, may have served as a vault for storing cider, which Pattee is known to have made. An aperture in the cavern, which romantics refer to as the "speaking tube," is so placed as to have been an ideal channel to carry cider pressed on the stone into containers stored within the cavern.

Summing up the work of this expedition, Hugh Morrison of Dartmouth spoke for the Early Sites Foundation when he wrote that "it has not yet succeeded in determining the purposes of the structures. It believes that study of other stone structures in New England will probably be most fruitful in answering this question."

An experienced Connecticut amateur thinks differently. Frank Glynn devoted the 1958 digging season to an exploration of the site's ground plan, and says that "it looks as though the plan is going to compare very closely with the plans of late Neolithic and Bronze Age oracle-sanctuaries from the Mediterranean area." His study, still in progress, is focused largely on geological clues. "Perhaps the most dramatic single example," he has said, "is the highly advanced weathering of the cut surfaces of the groove in the sacrifice table. These are so far decomposed that it is no longer possible to see the original tool marks. Comparison of this phenomenon with the cutting of names of the oldest settlers on similar granite in the cemetery a mile to the east indicates a totally different order of weathering."

In his preliminary excavations, Glynn also turned up artifacts he considers highly significant. "In June 1958 we recovered the first sherd of primitive pottery. It is coarse, soft-paste, fabric impressed—the size of your thumbnail. Most interesting are the hundreds of fragments of what Vescelius called 'bricks.' There are many fragments of fired, eighteenth- and nineteenth-century brick at the site in higher levels. Another type occurs most numerously in lower levels. It is sun-dried, hand-shaped, and quite thin; like adobe from the Southwest or the ancient bricks to be found from Portugal to India. They cannot by any stretch of the imagination be attributed to a nineteenth-century New England farmer."

In other words, the casebook on the discovery of America is still open. Hundreds of sites remain to be brought to light for the first time or to be explored with greater care. There is, for example, a carving on a rock at Westford, Massachusetts, which had been interpreted by William Goodwin as representing an eleventh-century Norse sword. However, when the Westford ledge was

Frank Glynn inspects carving of medieval knight after clearing away earth that had covered bedrock. Outlines of the carving have been traced in chalk.

completely exposed by Frank Glynn, there appeared a life-size carving of a man in medieval armor. The shield was emblazoned with a crescent, a star, a medallion, and a ship with furled sails. On the sword hilt a falcon spread its wings. After making careful drawings and a plaster cast of these impressions in the rock, Glynn sent his data to Dr. T. C. Lethbridge of the University Museum of Archaeology and Ethnology, Cambridge, England.

The British archaeologist (who is the Honorary Keeper of Anglo-Saxon Antiquities) identified the heraldry on the shield as that of the Orkney Sinclairs, lieges of the Norwegian throne in the fourteenth century. In collaborating with Dr. Lethbridge, Glynn turned up, in the Venetian narratives of Nicolo and Antonio Zeno, the story of a voyage to the Western Atlantic led by the first Earl of Orkney. "If we went on an expedition," Glynn reasons, "we

Glynn's drawing of carving shown on previous page.

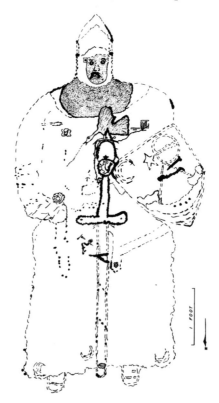

wouldn't take an undertaker and a tombstone cutter along, but we would have an armorer to repair our weapons." Glynn thinks it possible that the carving on the ledge near Westford memorializes the death of a fourteenth-century knight, that it was punched out in stone with the same tools a hammerer might have used to decorate a breastplate. If he is right in his conjecture, he may have unearthed still another clue to join the others which may some day add up to more definite knowledge of pre-Columbian visits to America. The carving Glynn found lies just off the Merrimack River, on the water route to North Salem's strange stone structures. What, if any, significance there is in this may be one of the problems to be solved by a dedicated archaeological amateur of the future.

Dozens of amateur archaeologists have long been fascinated with another carved rock in the Taunton River at Assonet Neck, just across from Dighton, Massachusetts. On this "mighty *Rock*, on a perpendicular side whereof by a River, which at High Tide covers part of it, there are very deeply Engraved . . . *odd Thoughts* about them that were here before us. . . ."

The words are Cotton Mather's, from *The Wonderful Works of God Commemorated*, published in 1690. Mather is describing what has come to be known as Dighton Rock, a brownstone petroglyph which has dazzled many an erudite observer. The "strange Characters" which Mather could not read were explained in 1781 by Count Antoine Court de Gebelin as telling of the voyage of ancient Carthaginian sailors who spent a friendly visit with the Indians on Mount Hope Bay. There have been other explanations, equally wild. Not long after the Frenchman's translation, a Harvard scholar announced he had found on Dighton Rock, written in Phoenician letters, the ancient Hebrew words for "king," "idol," and "priest." Another hopeful scholar saw here a message left by an expedition from Tyre and Judah, written in the second

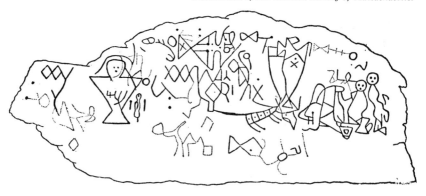

Above is the Dighton Rock inscription as it was sketched in 1834. Below, the same inscription has been given a few additional lines in the center, causing a Danish scholar to conclude that the words "Nam Thorfinn" had been carved on the rock.

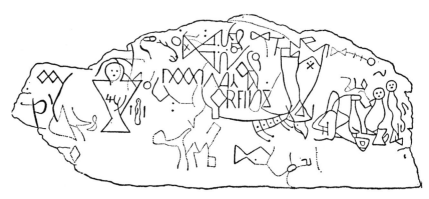

month of the tenth year of King Solomon's reign.

Again, however, it was the defenders of the Norse theory who brought furor to Dighton Rock. In 1837, five years after the death of Champollion, who had deciphered the hieroglyphs, a Dane named Carl Christian Rafn published a book called *Antiqvitates Americanae.* In it he said that he had been able to decipher from the man-made scratches on Taunton River sandstone the name of Thorfinn Karlsefni, the viking. Rafn and his associate, Finn Magnusen, contended that the rock described Karlsefni's life in Vinland, including a battle with an enemy called the "Skrellings."

Dighton Rock, wrote Rafn, announced that "Thorfinn and his 151 companions took possession of this land."

Few have doubted that the mysterious Dighton inscriptions were carved by men, but, because the tide keeps the rock partly submerged, many have wondered why any stonecutter would have chosen to stand in water above his knees when there are various near-by rocks more accessible. The archaeological explanation, surely, was pointed out at Saugus. Tide levels have risen a foot each century, making it reasonably certain that the man who so laboriously engraved the Dighton message had firm, dry footing while he did his work.

It is much less than certain, of course, that the engraver was a Norse. The Rafn theory, about which we will hear more, was dealt an almost lethal blow after Edmund B. Delabarre, a Brown University professor, purchased a Dighton summer home in 1912. Delabarre proved that Rafn had doctored the drawings he had been given of the inscriptions, that he had arbitrarily added lines to force the carvings to tell the story he wanted to believe. "There is a pleasure," Delabarre wrote, "in seeing uncertainties and irregularities resolve themselves into definite form, and the forms take on connected and acceptable meaning."

It was a statement he was to find true of himself. For thirty-three years Delabarre gave all the time he could to the Dighton mystery, and one day he, too, saw "uncertainties and irregularities resolve themselves into definite form." As he was choosing pictures for a book he had written on the subject, his gaze became fixed on a photograph he had examined a hundred times. "It may well be imagined with what astonishment," he said later, "I saw in it clearly and unmistakeably the date 1511. No one had ever seen it before, on rock or photograph; yet once seen, its genuine presence on the rock cannot be doubted."

Then, along with the date, Delabarre made out the emblazoned shield of the Kingdom of Portugal, and the Latin message: "Miguel Cortereal, by the will of God, here leader of the Indians."

Cortereal? Delabarre dug back into medieval history. João Vaz Cortereal was a Portuguese official who had two sons. Tradition said that João himself had sailed to Newfoundland and Labrador in 1472, when Columbus was still a Genoa weaver. And it is a matter of historic fact that João's son Gaspar made a similar voyage in 1501. After sending two ships home while he turned his flagship southward from Nova Scotia, Gaspar was never heard from again. His brother Miguel, the following year, went out to look for him, and he too was lost—until Edmund Delabarre saw his name, faintly, in the long debated rock on the Taunton River. Needless to say, Delabarre was decorated by the Portuguese government. As for the rock itself, it has been assigned a place on higher ground as the chief attraction of a new park just off the Fall River-Boston Expressway.

The fate of Rhode Island's Newport Tower, another object of Carl Christian Rafn's attention, is somewhat different. It has been summed up succinctly by that indefatigable New Englander Robb Sagendorph, publisher of *The Old Farmer's Almanac* and *Yankee Magazine*: "The most controversial building in America is one of the least impressive structures you ever saw. It is a squat, ungraceful cylinder of lime-mortared fieldstone, twenty-six feet high, with semicircular arches between eight chunky columns, and no roof, standing in the middle of Newport in a small park. There are a few small unframed windows scattered seemingly at random in the part above the arches, and these, combined with numerous niches on the inside, make it an admirable shelter for Newport pigeons, which is its only function at the present time."

Sagendorph wrote in 1954: "There is nothing grand in its proportions, nothing romantic in its location, no sign hinting at unusual origin; and yet this little stone ruin is said by some, and vehemently denied by others, to verify definitely perhaps one of the greatest and most intangible of all our legends—that the Vikings colonized America. For more than a century now, an occasionally scholarly, often fantastic, usually bitter dispute has raged about the old round tower. Over one hundred books, articles and pamphlets have attempted to throw light on its origin and purpose. The Irish, the Portuguese, the Dutch and even the ancient Druids have been suggested as the builders; but there have actually been only two theories that hold water—the Norse and the Colonial."

The Norse theory dates back to Carl Christian Rafn.

In gathering material for *Antiqvitates Americanae*, the Danish scholar had for years been in correspondence with Dr. Thomas H. Webb, secretary of the Rhode Island Historical Society, receiving suggestions about all sorts of unexplained curiosities in New England. It was not until 1839, however, that Webb called Rafn's attention to the Newport site, and he cast grave doubt on the popular tradition that the tower had been built in 1675 by Governor Benedict Arnold (great-grandfather of the Revolutionary turncoat). Webb had persuaded himself that the stone structure belonged to "the Vinland Scandinavians" and, to get Rafn's expert corroboration of his theory, he sent two drawings of the tower, the work of Frederick Catherwood, who had already published his sketches of Thebes, Karnak, and Luxor and was about to take off with John Lloyd Stephens to make the great Mayan discoveries in Central America. Rafn was enthused. He issued a supplement to *Antiqvitates Americanae* in which he attempted to prove that Newport's old round monument was indeed more than "my Stone-built wind-miln," as Governor Arnold had described it in his will; the building, Rafn asserted, had been erected in the twelfth century by Eric, Greenland's Bishop of Gardar, as a church.

For almost ten years the viking theory flourished. Newporters welcomed the thought that theirs was the site of the first Christian edifice in America. Longfellow used the tower as a setting for his romantic poem, "The Skeleton in Armor." But there were those who remained unconvinced and they worked persistently to prove that the architecture was actually an imitation by Arnold of a windmill located in the vicinity of Arnold's English birthplace. The debate continued for a century. Then in 1948, after an entire book (*Newport Tower*, by Philip A. Means) had been devoted to the subject, the Preservation Society for Newport County and the Society for American Archaeology persuaded city authorities to permit a dig under the direction of William S. Godfrey, Jr. Carrying out excavations in 1948 and 1949, Godfrey found under the tower's foundations the imprint of a colonial heel and a number of seventeenth century artifacts in a bed of brown-clay fill passing under four of the supporting columns. His conclusion was that the odd structure could not have been built before the English settlement of Rhode Island.

There is a word for the art of not being fooled: it is hermeneutics, the science of interpretation. No archaeologist can afford to overlook the necessity for skill in hermeneutics. Yet our field is spotted with embarrassments. One has only to mention the infamous Piltdown hoax, the "Dawn Man of Civilization" so successfully concocted by the English coroner Charles Dawson that it fooled experts for decades. Skill at hermeneutics might also have helped when the Cardiff giant was exhumed on a farm in New York's Onondaga Valley, causing even Ralph Waldo Emerson to pronounce it "beyond my depth, very wonderful and undoubtedly ancient." The giant, of course, turned out to be a statue in gypsum, carved by a Chicago stone cutter the year before its "discovery."

Perhaps the greatest challenge ever encountered by the science of hermeneutics—greatest at least in its quality of seesawing doubt—is the Kensington Rune Stone to which Hjalmar Holand has dedicated fifty years; Holand has related this rune to the Norse theory that still clings to the Newport Tower. For fifty-three weeks in 1948 and 1949 the stone was displayed in the Smithsonian Institution, its runic inscription describing the ordeal of a Norse party which had traveled as far inland as what is now Kensington, Minnesota.

Translated, the inscription read:

8 Swedes and 22 Norwegians on an exploration journey from Vinland westward. We had our camp by 2 rocky islets one day's journey north of this stone. We were out fishing one day. When we came home we found 10 men red with blood and dead. ÅVM save us from evil. We have 10 men by the sea to look after our ships, 14 days' journey from this island. Year 1362.

Since 1907 it has been Holand's theory that Magnus, King of

Front view and edge view of Kensington Stone.

ᛒᛋᚯᛏᛏᛦ:ᚼᛡ:ᚠᚠᛋᚼᚱᚱᚤᛏᛏ:ᛒᛡ:
ᛁ:ᚼᛒᚦᚷᛏᚦᛐᛆᚠᚷᚱᛈ:ᚠᚱᛡ:
ᚤᛁᛏᚠᚷᛏᛈᛡᚠ:ᚤᛐᛆᛏ:ᛡᛁ:

ᛏᚷᚦᛏ:ᛐᛉᚷᛏᚱ:ᚤᛏᚦᛋᚠ:ᛆᛐᚠᚷᚱᛋᛏᛏ:
ᚦᚷᛡᛆ:ᚱᛁᛆᛏ:ᚼᚱᚱ:ᚠᚱᛡ:ᚦᛏᛏᛋᛆᛏᛏ:
ᚤᛁᛋᚤᚷᚱᛡᛡ:ᚠᛁᛆᛏᛏᛏᚦᛉᚤᛏᛉᛒᛏᛁᚱ:

ᚤᛁ:ᛡᛡᚤ:ᛏᛏᚤ:ᚠᛉᛏᛈ:ᚤᛉᛏᚱᚯᚦᛏ:
ᛉᚠ:ᛒᛐᛡᚦᛋᛏᛁ:ᚦᛏᚦᛋᛆᚠᛘ:
ᚠᚱᛉᛏᛐᛆᛏ:ᛉᚠᛋᛁᛐᛐᚤ:

ᛏᛉᚱᛋᛈᛋᚤᛉᛏᛆᛋᚤᛏᛋᛏᛉᚤᛏᛏᛋᛉᛏᛋᛆᛏ:
ᛉᛒᛏᛁᚱ:ᚤᛡᚱᛏᛋᛆᛁᛒᛋᛐᛒᛋᛉᛉᛋᚱᛁᛆᛏ:
ᚠᚱᛡᚤ:ᚦᛏᛏᛡᛋᚯᛏᛋᛉᛏᚱᛋᛐᛁᛁᚠ:

The runic message on the Kensington Stone.

Norway, Sweden, and Skaane, sent an expedition to Greenland in 1354 to save the Christian church. The party is said to have wandered into Hudson's Bay, then down the Nelson River to Lake Winnipeg, from there via the Red River of the North to a Minnesota lake and then to what is now a swamp near Kensington. Menaced by Indians, the survivors of this odyssey are purported to have risked time which might have been valuable in escaping their enemies by sitting down and laboriously carving a message on two sides of a stone approximately two and a half feet high, sixteen inches wide, and between five and six inches thick.

This petrograph was unearthed in 1898 by a farmer named Olaf Ohman when he rooted out a ten-inch aspen on his land. Within six months the stone had been dismissed by several scholars as "a modern joke" and as "a crude fraud." Then a decade later there came a report giving credence to the inscription. The long controversy which followed involved runic scholars in various parts of Europe and the United States, as well as geologists, historians, and sculptors. The stone has been praised and vilified in book after book. A spokesman for the Smithsonian once called it "probably the most important archaeological object yet found in North America." Yet it is almost certainly a hoax perpetrated by a Minnesota farmer in 1898 and avidly fostered since 1907 by a man who wants too much to believe in bogus evidence of pre-Columbian visitors to America. The *coup de grâce* which finished the Kensington Rune Stone was delivered by Eric Moltke, runologist of the Danish National Museum: "We have before us a rune-stone which used symbols—j and ö—which were not invented until circa 1550, and the stone is dated 1362!"

Whether Hjalmar Holand has been jarred by a deduction as arresting as this one I do not know, but as recently as the spring of 1958 he had published an entirely separate theory under the title: *Nicholas of Lynn; A Pre-Columbian Traveler in North America*. In it he tells of the voyage in 1360 of Friar Nicholas of Lynn, England, to sub-Arctic shores of Canada, a visit for which Holand cites corroboration in Old Norse accounts.

An English cleric, a Scottish earl, an Irish bishop, a stone beehive maker, Venetian navigators, Scandinavian sea rovers: who discovered America? Nobody knows—yet.

8

Sundays in the Dirt

FROM THE TIME of my first Sundays in the dirt at Walden Pond, I have been intrigued by sites that did not seem to warrant full scale excavation. Such sites exist wherever man has settled in the United States. They may be no more mysterious than cellar holes reclaimed by nature or the faint hint of an abandoned wagon road in a field or a forest.

In the study of such sites, the digger is aided by history, of course, for there is usually some sort of written record from which to draw guidance. Through documents, letters, journals, and even newspapers we know a good deal about events in America during the seventeenth century, to cite just one time span. Enough has been written to give us a reasonably clear picture. But significant details are too often missing. Sometimes they are found in a bundle of letters in a gloomy attic, but more often they are completely out of sight, buried in the ground through negligence or expediency.

I have spent many weekends following archaeological trails which never could lead to world-shaking discoveries. One of them took me to Dogtown Common, the hilltop village in the heart of Cape Ann which was abandoned when the last inhabitant was taken away to the poorhouse. Dogtown hasn't changed in a hundred years. The description written in the last half of the nineteenth century by Thomas Wentworth Higginson is just as apt today: "Three miles inland we found the hearthstones of a vanished settlement . . . an elevated table-land overspread with great boulders as big as houses and encircled with a girdle of green woods and another girdle of blue sea. I know of nothing like that gray waste of boulders. It is a natural Salisbury Plain, of which icebergs were the druidic builders. In that multitude of monsters there seems a sense of suspended life; you feel as if they must speak and answer to each other. . . ."

Early settlers of Cape Ann chose this high land as insurance against pirates, but the small community ceased to prosper after it was bypassed by a road connecting Rockport and Gloucester; most of the original settlers moved down the hill. By the turn of the eighteenth century only a few widows of sea captains were left—each with a huge dog to protect her from the collection of weird vagrants who had established squatter's rights in the abandoned houses. When the widows died, their dogs ran wild, and the derelict community, as a result, became known as Dogtown.

Some of the squatters were believed to be expert in black art. Queen of the witches was Tammy Younger, whose house became a mecca for sailors eager to have their fortunes told. Near by lived Aunt Becky Rich, who sold what she called a "dire drink." Sammy Masson, dressed in a shawl and a long apron over his trousers, read the future in coffee grounds. In a sod hut known as "The

Boo," Granther Stannard functioned as the cobbler and dentist for the squatters, and not far from him was the shanty of Peg Wesson, who was said to ride a broomstick.

In 1814 only six of the original sixty houses were still standing. Black Neil Finson lived in one after the other of these, moving only when the roof caved in. When the last house collapsed he boarded the cellar over, and spent fruitless years digging for treasure he was sure lay buried.

With a Gloucester art teacher and two Rockport housewives who hoped to see a restoration of the settlement as it had looked in colonial times, I spent a day surveying the ruins that had once been the homes of Becky Rich or Colonel Pearce, or the school house presided over by Jane Day. Though the toppled stones were covered with rumcherries and cedar, and bayberry, blueberry, and elderberry bushes, the sites were so replete with artifacts that it required only digging with fingers to turn up glazed brown pottery and eighteenth century window glass. Almost completely camouflaged, however, was a mound we found in our search for a mill on Cape Pond Brook. Digging into this, we discovered the remnants of a dam, and with a little more probing I located a filled-in canal which led us to the site of a sawmill. When we returned to excavate, the blue-jeaned housewives dug as avidly as their young sons, and this amateur crew soon exposed the saw-mill's wheelpit, walled with field stones and buttressed with rocks. No one yet has gotten together the money to rebuild the village of Dogtown, yet the spare time excavation during those hot, mosquito-infested August days was the first step.

Another part-time excavation involved a New York publicity man and his wife, who became amateur archaeologists by chance. In the course of inspecting their newly purchased woods in Dutchess County, New York, Sue Zurhorst spotted some lilac blossoms and asked her husband to gather a bunch to take back to the city. Zurhorst pushed his way through a high thicket and stumbled across something that excited him far more than lilacs. "Look," he called, "somebody lived here before us!"

In the tangle of vegetation he had spotted the outlines of a fieldstone foundation, about fifteen by twenty feet. The next weekend he came back and cleared away some of the brush. Near the cellar hole, now clearly visible, was a gnarled apple tree, apparently several generations old. He found a second foundation. Then another. Eventually he brought to light the ruins of twenty structures. What was this? A forgotten village? Something about a giant boulder intrigued him. Cleaning it off Zurhorst became convinced that the grooves in the rock were ruts worn by wagon wheels. In the earth, his teen-age son found a broken iron kettle. Certainly, he thought, this was a colonial artifact. The family began to dig in earnest. They found the lid of a teapot, crockery sherds and bottle glass, clay pipe fragments, the hand-wrought head of a sledge hammer. Was this indeed a village that had escaped history?

Clues, if they existed, would be among recorded deeds or on old maps. In Poughkeepsie, Peekskill, and New York Zurhorst searched for the land grants to Dutch patroons. A map dated 1689 showed the area marked off as the "village of the Wappinger Indians." But no Indians Zurhorst had heard of ever dug cellars for their dwellings. He burrowed further into the archives. The Wappingers appeared to have abandoned this site when they had gone off to fight in the French and Indian War. A later map designated the area as "The Gore," a triangular piece of land whose ownership was disputed. More research revealed that in the middle of the eighteenth century settlers from Massachusetts and Connecticut had drifted west to the wooded land along the Hudson. They had established themselves as squatters on this wedge of no-man's land, digging cellars and putting up log cabins.

Sundays in the Dirt

Stealing out of the woods, they raided the valley estates for cattle. Zurhorst's study convinces him that these men were responsible for the invention of the word *cowboy*, used in the eighteenth century to mean rustler.

Scores of people have turned just as impulsively to digging. Dr. Wesley R. Coe, professor of zoology at Yale, one day recognized that the strange impressions in the great stone doorstep of his family's old homestead were the footprints of a dinosaur. The discovery sparked the prospect of finding other traces of prehistoric animal life on his central Connecticut farm. Twelve feet down, after five years of spare-time digging, he exposed an ancient riverbed swarming with dinosaur tracks of many different sizes.

On a Cape Cod holiday the painter Marstin Hodgin set off on a stroll among the sand dunes with his family, only to have his children spot fragments of clay pipes which had been brought to light by the ever-shifting sands. In no time the four Hodgins were on their hands and knees, digging like gophers. They found layers of bayberries hardened into cakes that must have been intended for seventeenth-century candle-making. They found leather heels pegged together with wood; and pieces of pottery and a bronze coin with a profile of William III which had been minted between 1695 and 1702.

More and more often in recent years I have found that people discovering historic sites are rightly turning to trained archaeologists for initial assessment, the process of surveying the site for accurate description of its potential. Some of these surveys belong among my own favorite Sundays in the dirt.

Easter weekend in 1957 found me on Cape Fear, North Carolina, at the request of Cornelius Thomas, who owns a large plantation not far from Wilmington. Accompanying me was Bob Wheeler, both of us setting our sights on the Thomas contention that Charles Towne, first English settlement on the Cape Fear

River, had been built and then abandoned on what is now the Thomas plantation. Cornelius Thomas and his son Neal had pursued the written record to establish that John Vassell, Surveyor General of Massachusetts Bay Colony and Barbados, had visited the Cape in May of 1664 and soon afterward, with Sir John Yeamans and a group of Massachusetts settlers, had founded Charles Towne. The archaeological problem was to determine whether underground evidence warranted extensive excavation on the plantation in the interest of unearthing the ruins of the settlement.

Within minutes, through only superficial examination of the terrain adjacent to the nineteenth-century Thomas house, it was apparent that the foundations of other structures would be found by digging. As I left the car on arrival I walked under canopies of Spanish moss and apple blossoms to the side of the white-pillared house. There, in the twilight, I noticed immediately a slight settling in the lush lawn not more than sixty feet from the mansion. This almost imperceptible depression was at least thirty feet square and was in perfect alignment with a small smokehouse Thomas believed to be the oldest standing building in North Carolina. I began to probe here with one of my rods and in about five minutes had traced a buried brick wall and established two of its corners. When the plantation owner came out and stood above this foundation still camouflaged by the lawn, he said that he had never dreamed of its existence. Yet when we dug the next morning, we exposed a well-made brick-walled cellar. Even more interesting to both Wheeler and myself was the coral I found when I had gotten up at sunrise to take pictures. The first chunks turned up when I probed at daybreak in an area close to the plantation canal that runs into the Cape Fear River. Later we spotted other coral pieces used as chinking in the smokehouse foundation. In this there were indications of early trade with Barbados and other parts of the West Indies, the coral having been imported by early

Sundays in the Dirt

colonists who lacked native lime for the making of mortar and plaster.

In another near-by section that day we located the sites of three two-family houses, finding bushels of fragments of roofing tile of a type that one colonial expert had asserted was not used after the seventeenth century. Unfortunately, our subsequent research showed that the roofing tile was being made and sold up to the Revolutionary War. This fact made it impossible to use the tiles as proof that the ruins we uncovered had been built in the first years of the English on the Carolina seaboard. Indeed, buildings with such pantile roofs might have been erected as slave quarters at Clarendon after it became a plantation in the 1720's. Most of the artifacts we found at these sites were readily recognized as belonging to the nineteenth and early twentieth centuries; we hit upon nothing which proved to belong to the era of the lost town's settlement. While this weekend survey did not reveal conclusive evidence of seventeenth-century occupation on the Thomas plantation, it did prove that the site warranted further archaeological exploration.

When he is a specialist in Americana, an archaeologist may often be asked to decide whether or not a historic site warrants restoration as a public monument. A case in point began when I received a request from a Pennsylvania oil man to examine an old structure located beside a stream on his property. He told me that if digging provided proof that the building figured in the Revolutionary War he would erect a reconstruction based on my findings. He welcomed the possibility of making a contribution to the history of his country—if underground evidence should warrant it. Excavations were conducted along the easterly wall of the stone building, exposing the base of the mill dam. Under an accumulation of rubble more than four feet deep, I found broken refractory brick, pieces of graphite crucibles, and ashes of anthracite coal used in an industrial hearth which had smelted non-ferrous metals. Opening a stoned-up arch in the building took us beneath a concrete floor to another mass of industrial ashes and clinkers. All this was late-nineteenth-century evidence, proving conclusively that the existing building had no association with the Revolution. The decision, therefore, was that there was not sufficient interest to justify a reconstruction.

A survey which took even less time—and had more promising results—followed a request that I inspect, and recommend ways to preserve, the Old Town Mill in New London, Connecticut. The president of the local historical society had written that the existing structure, built a few years after the Revolution, was the fourth or fifth building to have stood on the site of a mill erected by John Winthrop, Jr., in 1650. Under the mill, with my probe rod and very little digging, I traced the foundation of a smaller and earlier mill. The stonework had been buried late in the eighteenth century, and a larger structure erected over it. Careful excavation was all that was necessary to reveal the first site of industrial activity in this region.

More and more people are being persuaded to show interest in this kind of buried heritage. Typical is Ralph Grayson Schwarz, of Bethlehem Steel, who had been enthusiastic about the ironworks excavations at Saugus, and who in 1957 asked me to supervise a weekend dig in Bethlehem, Pennsylvania, on the grounds of Moravian College. Considerable historical research has been under way here for years under the auspices of the Annie S. Kemerer Museum and Historic Bethlehem, Inc., which hope to restore as much as possible of the community as it looked in the eighteenth and early nineteenth centuries. Ralph Schwarz's first interest, as far as digging was concerned, was in an island once used by the Moravians for relaxation. Moravian maps showed its general location, but a branch of the stream had been filled in, thus covering up the island. How deeply it was buried was not known. To find out, Ralph organized a group of a dozen volunteers, and Bob Wheeler and I drove to Bethlehem to lend a hand.

This again was to be an archaeological survey to determine whether or not the site warranted a full scale excavation. In a day and a half of digging, it became evident that more than fourteen feet of fill covered the island. In addition, the bed of the Monocacy Creek, which the Moravians had originally diverted to form the island, had been raised to a point higher than the island's surface. Our digging made it apparent that an accurate restoration was

Test pits went deep into ground in search of Wunder Island on Moravian College campus.

Richness of soil in buried apothecary garden is shown in the dark stratification at bottom of test pit.

impractical, if not entirely impossible, yet all of those who volunteered that weekend shared a sense of discovery. We now knew a great deal more about the buried island than the meager facts preserved in the historical record.

The following spring Wheeler and I again joined Schwarz for a second dig on the college grounds, this time locating the site of

Sundays in the Dirt

the apothecary gardens which had provided medicinal herbs for the Moravian pharmacy established in 1742. It had been planted in the days when mint, thyme, lavender, sage, marjoram, liquorice, and other plants had been referred to as "precious herbs" to heal the sick. Mandrake then was cultivated as a pain killer, a genus of figwort as a remedy for eye trouble, and mistletoe to cure epilepsy; the milk of lettuce was often prescribed for sleeplessness. The soil in which such drugs had thrived had been buried by many changes in the college campus.

On the lawn of one of the Moravian buildings, Bill Murtagh, who was the director of the Annie S. Kemerer Museum in Bethlehem, had had a grid of five-foot intervals staked out. Our volunteers gathered here in a downpour that lasted all day. Rain saturated the turf. I remember the way it clung like tiny pearls in the dark hair of Connie Donaldson and Lou Murtagh, Bill's wife, two of the most indefatigable of the volunteer wives. This crew rolled out tar paper to protect the lawn, and placed upon it all the sod and soil that was excavated. Their shovels helped to cut expert test pits. And under a two-foot layer of protective fill they found the reddish brown richness of the soil in which the eighteenth century "physick Garden" had been planted. We had dug until we hit natural, undisturbed earth. Immediately above this was the brown stratum which once had been cultivated. It was cleaner than the usual strata of human occupation; only a scattering of artifacts was found in it. A sample taken from this layer was analyzed by a geologist, who confirmed the fact that it was topsoil. It was still recognizable chemically, in spite of the fact that it had been buried and subjected to the leaching of rain trickling down through ashes and other fill soils for more than a century and a quarter. In this buried garden we found dark circular stains which contained the stringy remnants of rotting wood. These were post molds, last evidence of an arbor, or perhaps a fence. Picks and shovels this weekend had cut down to the land as it had been when the first Moravian settlers arrived in 1742.

Most communities have archaeological problems growing out of legends. These are the potential digs I like to think of as sitting ducks. Like the fabled escape tunnel in Woodbury, Connecticut, they lie waiting for amateurs with the will to use a shovel and follow the rules.

Woodbury's legend leads back, not surprisingly, to the era of the Revolutionary War. It concerns "the glebe house," an Episcopal minister's residence so named because it stood on glebe property—land donated to the parish. The legend tells us that the minister who lived here during the eighteenth century was so persecuted for his loyalty to George III that he devised an underground passage through which he could either escape or have food brought to him by sympathizers when he was besieged. A secret sliding-panel gave him access to the tunnel and was said still to have been workable in the twentieth century. Unsolicited letters recalled boyhood memories of entering it from the cellar or from just inside the front door. There were memories of passing through it to the other side of the road, and others to the effect that there had been a cave-in. No two accounts agreed in detail, but all insisted that investigation would firmly establish the existence of the secret passage.

The legend was so much a part of the environment of the community that it might have been in the better interests of entertainment to support it. But the need to know the facts persists, and I was asked in the summer of 1952 to help a former rector of the parish direct a dig. He had persuaded me to contribute several days of a vacation I was taking from the Saugus work, and I drove down to Woodbury on October 2, 1952, expecting to set to work at once with a crew of eager amateurs.

Sundays in the Dirt

Instead I found confusion. There was not a volunteer on the scene, and it was only after a round of telephoning that two high-school boys and two laborers were enlisted. The debaters, who had been so eager to have an active archaeologist pass judgment on their problem, now hung around to watch, as if they hoped to catch a glimpse of the ghosts of those who had walked in the glebe-house tunnel.

Before we put a hand to a shovel in Woodbury, however, I had first marshalled the data pertinent to the tunnel legend. One letter said that "about 1907 . . . after descending the cellar stairs we was able to move or slide a part of the petition [sic] on the left side of the cellar stairs that led us into a passage under the ground bearing northeast toward the street. After crawling some yards I came to the entrance to the real tunnel it was open for only a few feet and the dirt had caved in and rotten logs blocked the entrance. The thrill and satisfaction in seeing that entrance has never been forgotten as one of the exciting events of my boy hood days in this historic old town of Woodbury Conn."

Another letter reported that "during the years of 1910 to 1912 . . . I crawled through a tunnel from the northeast corner of the basement . . . as far as the road and came out under a small bridge. . . ." A third recalled a sliding panel immediately inside the front door through which "during the years of 1910 and 1911 . . . we entered the tunnel by stepping into a shallow shaft a few feet below the floor level. . . . I remember going into this tunnel . . . but do not know whether it was broken down at the road making further passage impossible. . . . The walls and ceiling of this tunnel, as near as I can recall, were shored up with logs and the tunnel itself must have been about four feet in width and depth."

All these accounts, written many years after the boyhood excursions, tended to suggest that there had indeed been something resembling a tunnel below the glebe house. So I laid out eight test trenches which would bisect any avenue of escape in the directions indicated in the letters—and more importantly in the direction of the houses known to have been occupied by the eighteenth century parishioners who were said to have been in league with the beseiged minister.

At a point nine and a half feet northeast of the east corner of the house I had the crew dig a pit. Pieces of brick and plaster were found to a depth of seventeen inches. Two feet down we hit natural clay, undisturbed by man, and at thirty-eight inches water began to seep in. Probe rod tests to a depth of six or seven feet also failed to find evidence of a tunnel. Following the same northeast line from the house we crossed the road and cut a trench eleven and a half feet long; here we found water six inches below the surface. On the second day of the dig we cut into the lawn beside the northeast wall of the house and found water forty inches below the undisturbed level. Three trenches on the third day brought us to the water running underground at the front of the house. All the test trenches were further explored with the deep-reaching probe rods, and at no point was there the slightest evidence of a tunnel. Only by digging a continuous trench to circle the house completely could I have been more certain that there had never been an underground escape route. Yet further digging was not called for because the slit trenches had bisected any line of escape between the position of the glebe house cellar and the locations of the Tory houses on the high ground.

But what gave boys in the early years of the twentieth century the idea that a Revolutionary War passage was there for them to traverse? Like all legends, the glebe-house story undoubtedly began with a kernel of fact. Perhaps in the years of colonial strife the Reverend Mr. John Rutgers Marshall did have a secret room, accessible through the cellar, in which he hid himself. My own

Sundays in the Dirt

169

Heavy mechanical equipment helped to uncover buried dam and site of factory at Dover, Massachusetts.

feeling is that it was more likely a cooling-cellar; the walls had disintegrated enough so that someone with an active imagination assumed that beyond the rubble might be a tunnel. Yet it may also be likely that Marshall's parishioners did have occasion to slip through the guards to bring him food. And as the story was told by one generation to another, some early yarn spinner introduced the tunnel aspect as an innocent embellishment. Any child might delude himself into believing that the crumbled walls of a basement recess blocked the kind of underground passage which so appealed to him.

Restored dam at Dover after completion of the dig.

One backyard exploration that had no mysterious overtones came about as the result of a talk on the Saugus Ironworks I was asked to give before the Dover Historical Society in Massachusetts. Miss Amelia Peabody, who was in the audience, told me that on her Dover farm was a breached dam that once had retained a mill pond. My discovery of the water wheel under Central Street had aroused her curiosity. Was there the chance of a similar find on her mill stream?

When I arrived at her farm, I found a great mound of rubble covered with February snow. Here the giant stones of the dam had

Sundays in the Dirt

spilled down, piling up on the site of the water wheel and mill, and leaving a breach through which ice-encrusted water flowed from the pond above. With two diggers and a mechanical crane with a clam-shell bucket, the picture soon changed. In spite of days when the thermometer registered six below zero, we were able to clear away the dam rubble, including the three-quarter-century-old trees that had grown in it, and to cut through the frozen soil to find the stone wheel pit and a large section of a thirty-six-foot overshot water wheel at the bottom. We had unearthed the site of the Dover Union Iron Company, its furnace and warehouse foundations still sharply outlined in the original soil. As spring came, we began to rebuild the dam. A test pit had determined that the original base of the dam had been sunk six feet below the surface. It was twelve feet thick at the base, and upon this we built up the flat-surfaced stones which had formed the facing. They had been laid without mortar at the time the dam was erected, but to stabilize the reconstruction I had ninety-eight yards of concrete and pea-stone gravel delivered. This was poured in on the pond side along with many tons of stones, leaving the appearance of dry masonry on the face. Stone by stone we put the dam back together again, and it stands today twenty-three-and-a-half feet above the floor of the mill which abutted it. The forty-foot wheelpit was restored, its stone sides reaching twenty feet below the mill floor; high above, a stream of water shoots through the spillway just as it did when the giant wheel powered this early Massachusetts industry.

The Dover site, Woodbury's glebe house, and Dogtown Common—all are clear demonstrations of the ways in which archaeology can be put to use to solve local historical problems. "Historians," according to Thomas Jefferson Wertenbaker of Princeton University, "have depended too much on manuscript evidences. . . . Perhaps the day is not too distant when the social historian, whether he is writing about the New England Puritans, or the Pennsylvania Germans, or the rice planters of Southern Carolina, will look underground, as well as in the archives, for his evidence."

9

Burials and Vanished Tepees

As a boy in nineteenth-century South Dakota, Matthew Oldham found nothing but trouble every time his father told him to plow the south forty. There was a wide ditch cutting across that field and it curved into the adjoining pasture. Matt used to begin cursing as he hit the ridge. It seemed impossible to keep a straight furrow as he drove the team down the shallow slope and up the other side; as the plow hit bottom it would lurch and throw the handles out of his struggling grip. Not until he'd grown old and retired did he find out what caused all the trouble.

All those years the Oldhams had been trying to cultivate a moat which had been dug to protect an Arikara Indian village, a fact they might never have known but for a vast governmental dam-building program. The projected dams would flood large areas, and the program underscored the need for salvage archaeology. In

1947 a survey team from the Smithsonian Institution came to South Dakota and found that erosion and dust storms had partially camouflaged the moat, that originally it had been fifteen feet deep and had encircled a log stockade. The saucer-shaped depressions in the near-by pasture—which Matt's father had assured him were buffalo wallows—actually contained the decayed stumps of wooden uprights, once the framework of Arikara earth lodges. Digging within the circles outlined by the post molds, the Smithsonian crew turned up the timbers of fallen roofs, potsherds and grinding stones, arrowheads by the peck, and the cold hearths of the vanished Arikaras.

Four years later, when the Federal River Basin Surveys swung into concentrated action, Robert B. Cumming, Jr., arrived at the Oldham farm to begin a second excavation. The Indian village site had created so much interest among the citizens of near-by Platte that Elmer Gardner, former mayor of the town, volunteered to join the Cumming crew. Not only that, he lined up seven friends in their sixties and seventies to serve as diggers. Cumming reported later that he never had better helpers: "They moved more dirt than the average team of husky young college students." Under Cumming's direction, the history-minded oldsters finished excavating the fortified village, determining that it had been built about 1700; beneath it they found vestiges of an earlier community, dating back to the Middle Ages.

Forty feet of water, backed up thirty miles behind the huge Fort Randall dam, now covers those sites, and never again will there be a chance for an archaeologist to learn more about the various people who lived on this stretch of the Missouri River before the white man came. Areas all over America have suffered similar fates. In the vast water-control program creating 241 reservoirs, government figures indicate that 4,281 points of Indian occupation are being inundated for all time, and only through such accelerated programs of co-operative archaeology will previously unknown facts about Indian life be uncovered and preserved. In the seven-hundred-mile segment of the Missouri which lies between Omaha and the Montana border, six hundred villages have been excavated, some of them containing several hundred Indian dwellings. Archaeology, because of this emergency program, has revised the notion that this region was inhabited exclusively by migrant warriors.

New facts about the Indians are being uncovered every day— and the vast majority of this digging is being done by amateurs. I'm reminded, for instance, of a discovery made in 1954 by a group of my friends in Massachusetts led by Maurice Robbins. For weeks that summer they had been carefully excavating a site on the northern shore of Lake Assawompsett near Lakeville, a few miles inland from Buzzard's Bay. One day, thirty inches below the modern surface, they unearthed part of a weapon which appeared to be identical with the famed Folsom Point, found lodged between the ribs of a bison extinct for 10,000 years. Carbon-14 tests have substantiated the belief that the ancient hunter who felled the bison was roaming New Mexico in 8000 B.C., and Maurice Robbins might have jumped to the conclusion that Folsom man was in Massachusetts at the same time.

Yet much as he may have wished his Lake Assawompsett excavation to be equally important, Maurice and his fellow amateurs clung to the cautious approach. "While it is true that a Folsom-like point was taken from this site," he reported to the Archaeological *Newsletter*, "it was found at some distance from charred logs and was not in association with them. . . . Should the date of the logs prove to be respectably ancient one might assume such an association, but such an assumption would be nothing more than an educated guess. Surely nothing so important as the date of entry of man into the northeast could be logically based thereon." In the earth, though, Robbins and his colleagues did find the well-trodden floor of a circular lodge and traces of six other dwellings, many stone hearths, two crematories and hundreds of stone tools and dishes. Burned bones were established as being those of human beings by Dr. J. O. Brew, director of the Peabody Museum of Archaeology and Ethnology at Harvard. Charcoal from one of the firepits of this nomadic village showed an age of 4,320 years, plus or minus 250, when it was tested by Carbon 14. Nothing so far turned up has proved as old as Folsom Man. "It would seem," Maurice Robbins summed up, "that the Boylston Street fishweir is still the best indication of the age of New England man."

Boston's Boylston Street became archaeologically famous in 1913 when construction workers for the Huntington Avenue subway inadvertently exposed some buried fish traps. Not until after World War II and the perfection of radiocarbon testing was it possible to interpret the age of the weirs. Though no one has yet provided an earlier date for the arrival of man in New England, the Boylston Street tests have indicated that he was in residence, and thriving, about 7,000 years ago. At this writing the dig at Lake Assawompsett has produced nothing to set this date back, but it does demonstrate one more contribution by amateurs to the slowly accumulating picture of prehistoric life throughout the country.

Though the terms are not precise and dating is still somewhat debatable, the prehistory of man in America is usually described as encompassing the Paleo-Indian, Archaic, Woodland, Mississippi, and Pueblo cultures. It was, thus, in the nomadic Paleo-Indian period that fishermen staked out the Boylston weirs, the same period that the flint projectile felled the bison found near Folsom, New Mexico. In the succeeding period, the Archaic—which began about 4000 B.C.—archaeology has found signs of community life, of basket-making, of stone implements and dishes, and even copper objects. The change from Archaic to Woodland culture began

Burials and Vanished Tepees

about 1000 B.C., when pottery was introduced and when men began to bury their dead under mounds of earth. As the Woodland phase progressed, the domestication of plants was begun, pottery-making became an art, and burial mounds began to take the form of effigies like that of Ohio's Great Serpent. Some time after the beginning of the Christian era, the tribal Mississippi culture developed throughout the east and the plains states, and in the Southwest there rose the civilization centered about the pueblos.

Non-professionals are active in all these periods. When the oldest known dwelling in southeastern United States was made a national monument in 1958, Carl F. Miller of the Smithsonian Institution pointed out that the "potentialities were discovered by members of the Chattanooga Archaeological Society, who drew my attention to the cave." This site, which lies three-quarters of a mile south of the Tennessee-Alabama border and about two miles west of the Alabama-Georgia line, is known as Russell Cave.

Though comparatively few ancient cave dwellings have been found in the United States, Paul Brown, LeBaron Pahlmeyer, Charles Peacock and J. B. Graham were sure they had made a consequential prehistoric find in Russell Cave, and they knew that trained archaeologists are constantly on the lookout for any ready-made shelter which might have been used by ancient man. In Bat Cave in New Mexico, in 1948, an expedition led by Herbert W. Dick discovered dried prehistoric plants ranging in date from 2500 B.C. to A.D. 500, and including specimens of primitive maize, the oldest ancester of corn on the cob. In a cave near Reserve, New Mexico, in dust so fine and thick as to require respirators, goggles, and artificial lighting, Dr. Paul S. Martin uncovered 3,500 specimens, including snares, bows and arrows, digging-sticks, kernels of dried corn, bean seeds, squash, pumpkins, bags, baskets, rush mats, whistles, cloth, rope, fur robes, feather blankets, hair nets, two hundred sandals, and a doctor's kit filled with herbs and primitive instruments. This site contained stratifications ranging from 2500 B.C. to A.D. 1300. Martin had spent years in search of a cave as protected and dry, for only an enclosure sealed off from normal fluctuations in temperature could preserve articles made of organic materials.

Carl Miller had a similar interest in Russell Cave after the four amateurs had called his attention to it. He found that it measured 107 feet across the mouth and penetrated into the hillside for 270 feet on a horizontal plane; its ceiling, as he discovered it, varied from twenty-three to twenty-eight feet above the hard dirt floor that had been packed by the feet of many generations of occupants. "Below its opening," Miller said in a magazine article, "flows a clear cold stream that disappears close by into another cavern. A fissure at the rear of the Indian's cave connects the two. Through the crack pours cool, natural air conditioning for hot summer days."

Like Martin, Miller had found a place to dig that had been set aside by nature as a unique archaeological storage vault. Because of the cave's ideal atmosphere, a grass-fibre basket filled with small charred seeds had not decayed although under seven feet of earth.

"Because the cave dwellers, instead of sweeping out their litter, buried it under fresh layers of earth, the story of their lives is as easily read as the rings of a tree," Miller wrote. "Gradually an area thirty feet square was peeled away in steps. With each six inches dug, time rolled backward. At the six-foot level a skeleton was found of a cave Indian who lived and died about 4,000 years ago. In another, more carefully made grave, a dog was buried with his ancient master. Near the fourteen-foot level, projectile points were found from the earliest Archaic period, as well as a stone pierced by a smooth man-made hole. This was identified as an *atlatl*, a primitive spear-throwing device whose name comes from the Aztecs."

Burials and Vanished Tepees

The dig at Russell Cave gave Miller what he called "a consecutive record of human occupancy from 6200 B.C. or earlier until about A.D. 1650." Charcoal from man-made fires found at the fourteen-foot level was dated by radioactive Carbon 14 as being 8,160 years old, plus or minus 300 years.

Conjectural outline added to fluted point found on Macon plateau.

Long before the Russell Cave discoveries, archaeologists were working at a near-by townsite where an occupation of 7,000 years duration was revealed. On the Macon Plateau in Georgia—through the excavation of temple and funeral mounds, a ceremonial lodge, and peripheral villages—an Indian community was unearthed whose culture was as advanced in some respects as any yet found north of Mexico. This dig beside the Ocmulgee River, on the outskirts of Macon, proceeded for twenty years. It began in 1933 as a Civil Works Administration project under the direction of Arthur R. Kelly, and later was sponsored by the Society for Georgia Archaeology and the Macon Chamber of Commerce. A dozen archaeologists were active here for varying periods, turning up among thousands of relics a fluted projectile point dropped by a migrant hunter more than 5,000 years before the Christian era; in the course of the dig they found the record of three separate occupations.

The first people who settled on this high riverside plateau were hunters and shellfish eaters. The excavations here show that they

There was little scholarly interest in Indian mounds in the early nineteenth century. Pioneers treated the mounds as they saw fit, sometimes building houses on them.

gathered river mussels, and killed deer and other game; their women collected nuts, roots, and berries. In the beginning, they cooked by barbecuing or stone-boiling in skin-lined pits. Later, stone vessels were made of talc, and finally pottery was introduced. They developed as farmers, growing squashes, beans, corn, and tobacco. Now their pottery was elaborately decorated, and they began to build earthen mounds for religious and burial purposes.

Archaeological evidence indicates that, during the most civilized occupation, one temple mound was reserved for the dead. There, it appears, the villagers erected scaffolds on which bodies were aged until the bones could be easily cleaned. There are indications that elaborate funeral rituals for important personages took place in a wooden temple on top of the mound, and interment was some-times made in sunken wooden tombs. After such occasions the mound platforms were carefully covered with clean sand, and new and larger temples replaced the old.

When excavators arrived at the site in the 1930's, they found the

Burials and Vanished Tepees

great funeral mound measured 100 by 230 feet and rose twenty-five feet from the ground. Three sloping sides were eroded and pitted, and the fourth—cut away in construction of the Central of Georgia Railway—was almost vertical. Yet on the western slope there still remained an earthen stairway with brilliant red clay steps set into the slate-blue mound. The diggers found that this earthen pyramid was composed of seven construction levels, each containing burials of village leaders. The original mound had been increased in height at six successive time intervals. Each level, made of earth carried in baskets from a pit outside the village, was covered with a layer of clay, perhaps to minimize erosion.

More than a hundred burials were found in the funeral mound, and burial offerings remained in more than half of these. There were two log tombs. In the clay exterior of the fifth level was a

Archaeologists estimate that 1,000,000 basket-loads of earth were required to build the Great Temple Mound at Ocmulgee. At the right of the house in the background is a much smaller mound. Both mounds were built between A.D. 900 and A.D. 1100.

Fourteen clay steps, buried under later construction, led up the west slope of the Ocmulgee funeral mound.

This log tomb was unearthed at Ocmulgee, during National Park Service excavations. The face-down position may indicate a burial in which reassembled bones were wrapped in animal skin or matting.

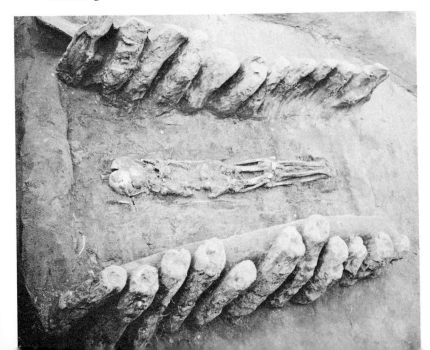

grave containing the most interesting trophies of the entire mound; the offering included two large copper medallions fluted and shaped to resemble a scallop shell, which served, it is thought, as a part of a chieftain's headdress. Beside these shimmering metal "sun discs" were two jawbones of a puma which had been sheathed

Masses of shell beads found in Ocmulgee graves have been interpreted as indicating the importance of the dead person.

in hammered copper, as well as the remains of a fur piece. Reproductions of these funerary gifts, on display in the Ocmulgee National Monument museum, now provide quick insight to Indian craftsmanship of a thousand years ago.

The Ocmulgee excavations also revealed the floor and earthen foundations of a ceremonial lodge occupying a circular area forty-two feet in diameter. Here forty-seven carefully carved earthen seats were well preserved, and facing these was a clay platform supporting three additional seats. Another excavated structure had been framed by a circle of abutting poles and contained an enormous fireplace; it was a sweathouse where steam was produced by throwing water on sizzling stones.

Sometime during the eleventh century this mound-building cul-

Excavation of one of eight earth lodges found at Ocmulgee. The fireplace is in the center, and at the right can be seen the ceremonial basins—one before each seat on the circular bench.

Copper "sun discs" and puma jaws sheathed in copper were found in a grave in the fifth level of the funeral mound at Ocmulgee. In a reconstruction at the Georgia national monument the four pieces are shown as part of a ceremonial headdress.

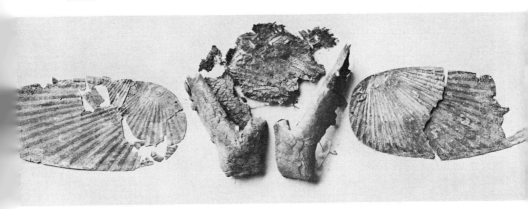

Indian potters in the southeast frequently sculptured bottles to resemble human beings. At the left is shown the top of a bottle which has a hole in the back of the head; the face is painted white, the body red, and the hair is the natural brown clay. On the right is a blank-face type with two semicircular ridges said to represent ears.

From the fourteenth to the seventeenth centuries Indians in southeastern U.S. made pipes in an astonishing variety of skillfully executed shapes, sometimes of clay and sometimes of soft stone.

This dancing figure is on display at Ocmulgee National Monument museum and was copied from an embossed copper plate found under a skull in a stone-lined grave near Cartersville, Georgia.

Stone celt found at Ocmulgee. The wooden handle is reconstructed from representatives found in other Southeastern Indian cultures.

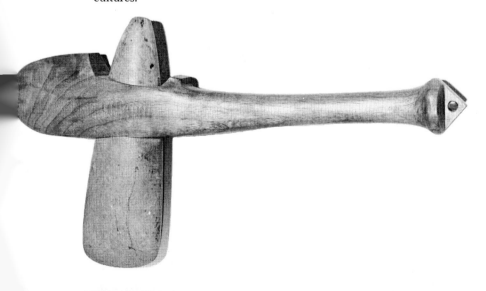

Mimbres pottery designs depict community life. At the left is an Indian "blanket party," at the right the harvesting of grasshoppers.

ture disappeared. Like the Mayas of Central America its fate is unknown. We must continue to dig in the area drained by the Mississippi and Ohio Rivers where there were other mound builders, and where clues to greater understanding may still be found.

There are, for example, scores of sites in the Middle West which belong to the Hopewell culture, the mound-building society so-named because it was identified first on the Hopewell farm in Hamilton County, Ohio. One of the largest concentrations of such mounds and village sites is in Jackson County, in southern Illinois, where amateur diggers are almost constantly active. On near-by bluffs and rocks the art work of even earlier Americans can be seen. Some are strange designs chiseled into flat stones and some are murals as vivid and interesting, though not as sophisticated, as the cave paintings of France and Spain. These primitive drawings of animals and birds, of mystic symbols, hand and foot prints, hunting parties and canoes, form an unfathomed trail across the continent. Scores have been seen in the wilderness reaching out from Lake Superior. When they were done, and why, is still unknown—

and we are gradually losing them because of erosion and other natural causes. Painted with a mixture of clays, animal fats, and rust-colored iron oxides from stream beds, they represent the oldest art in America, the first yearnings of Stone Age people to express themselves.

Surprisingly, perhaps, it is not the Stone Age that has had the most attention from Indian specialists. Since 1888, when the major cliff dwellings were discovered on Mesa Verde, there has been constant interest in the history of the Pueblo Indians who settled in the southwest shortly before the year A.D. 1. Much of the great interest here has been focused on the Classic Pueblo period which extended from A.D. 1050 to the beginning of the fourteenth century. Here archaeologists have been able to study urban communities and early American architecture, including houses with as many as a thousand rooms.

It is beyond the scope of this book to present an adequate description of the Pueblo towns and their inhabitants; the story is complex. Because the life was agricultural, the Pueblos developed

Painted rocks along the Gila River, in Arizona, sketched in the mid-nineteenth century.

Burials and Vanished Tepees

189

great ability in coaxing sustenance out of native plants. Cotton was known in the Pueblo world as early as 700 A.D. Pottery-making was an art, and some of the world's finest examples of ceramics come from the Classic period in New Mexico. Twelfth-century jewelry fashioned here of shell and turquoise inlay has been compared to the work of such Renaissance artisans as Benvenuto Cellini. The social and religious life was organized in small societies or clans, each of which had its own kiva—the ceremonial structure, usually round, found in such multiplicity in all the great houses.

Many of these multi-family dwellings were three stories tall and pushed out from the cliff three or four rooms deep, so that the caves which were occupied first became relegated to storage space. A typical room measured about six by nine feet, with a ceiling height of five feet eight inches; it had a doorway not more than three feet high and only half as wide; an opening or two in the front wall near the ceiling was designed to facilitate the escape of smoke, and a similar hole at the floor level furnished a draft.

Certainly, man moved to the cliffs for reasons of defense; many of these early apartment houses were raised high on the faces of perpendicular bluffs, and often they were fortified with defensive walls. The dwellings which the Pueblo people had occupied earlier were equally impressive, but were built of free-standing mortared walls of volcanic rock, rising on the tops of mesas or in the center of canyons.

When James A. Lancaster and Jean M. Pinkley excavated a Mesa Verde site in 1950, they found striking evidence of three occupations—a post and adobe village erected about A.D. 900 had been burned sometime between 975 and 1000 and replaced first by a single-coursed masonry pueblo, then a century later by a house with double-coursed walls. "The superimposed structures," they said, "are testimony to the continuing efforts expended by these people to improve their homes and enhance their religious edifices. . . . The story of Site 16 [as it is designated at Mesa Verde] is a story of human advancement, and as such this insignificant appearing ruin adds its bit to the history of man."

Any one of us may contribute to this gathering knowledge. It was a Negro cowboy named George McJunkin who led the experts to that arroyo near Folsom, New Mexico. He had noticed the gleam of white bones in a newly washed-out gully and when he climbed down for a closer look he found flints which looked like none he had ever seen. Reporting his find, the cowboy brought skeptical scientists to the site. The bones turned out to be bones of the straight-horned bison, a contemporary of mammoths and mastodons, an animal extinct since 8000 B.C., the flints were clearly the points of weapons hurled by an ice age hunter, and the find stood for many years as the earliest evidence of human occupation in the New World.

Thus to an amateur come chances to make contributions to archaeology. It may happen as humbly as it did for Edward Patterson in Sea Cliff, New York. He noticed a layer of clam shells in an eroded cliff on Garvey's Point, Long Island, and came to the conclusion that the shells could not have been left so far from the Sound without help from man. Patterson enlisted a few boys as helpers and began to excavate as a weekend pastime. His first finds led him to think that his shell midden had been left by the Matinecock tribe in the sixteenth century, but as his trenches went deeper he ran into pre-ceramic utensils which placed the lower layers of the shell heap in the Archaic Period. He had found the leavings of people who had settled on Long Island fifty years before the birth of Christ. These discoveries excited many local citizens, and the Nassau County Archaeological Society was formed as the result.

Information about the shellfish-eaters is still scanty, but it is known that about 5,000 years ago these early Americans discovered a new source of food in the lowly mussel, the clam, and the oyster. Thus they freed themselves from the multiple hardships of moving constantly to keep up with the game. They spread out along the coasts, along the Mississippi and Ohio Rivers. They discarded their empty shells on the ground, and the piles mounted as the decades passed. The bones of deer, bear, rabbit, turkey, and other wildlife were mingled with the shells whenever the diet was varied as the result of good hunting. Fragments fell among the shells as they chipped stone for darts and spears and household utensils; broken pottery was left where it fell.

The level of this refuse sometimes rose to great heights because men lived on top of the midden. Living-surfaces and hearths have been found not only on the ground below the pile, but at various levels; sometimes the shells are found to be almost pulverized by trampling. Some layers consist of nothing but clams, sometimes quahogs or oysters dominate a single stratum. In cases where shellfish have remained abundant, these garbage heaps grew monstrous—the largest so far reported in the United States is thirty feet high and extends over thirty-five acres; it is covered by top soil deposited by winds, and is disguised by trees and vegetation. Such a midden is a priceless record of the evolution of man in America. By cutting a profile trench through it we can see this record: on the bottom are the relics of people who had not yet learned to make pottery but who did make very crude weapons. We see next a layer in which there are utensils made of talc and soapstone, on top of this succeeding forms in the evolution of pottery, refinements in projectile points, and the development of other tools.

The vast shell heaps along the Damariscotta River in Maine had long been famous when I explored them in 1956. They had been known to white men as early as the ill-fated English colony established on the lower Kennebec River in 1607. For generations, scientists have been probing to find all the secrets they contain—at the same time that other men have tried to make them commercially

Pipe tomahawk made of malleable cast iron found at Damariscotta, Maine. The blade decoration shows a half moon, stars, and a bear on one side, on the other the outline of an Indian head.

Items of Indian trade found at Saugus included clay pipes, sometimes with the initials of Robert Tippet, fishhooks, jew's-harps, and brass spoons, some of which bore the trademark of three spoons in a circle (Fig. 5).

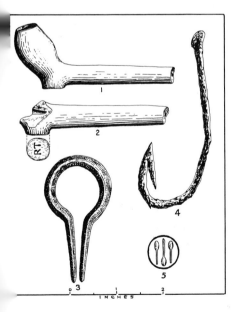

valuable. Hundreds of tons have been hauled away for paving walks and driveways, and two large factories were built in the nineteenth century in unprofitable attempts to turn the shells into lime. Despite this depletion, the piles that remain are awesome. A geologist reckoned that the great mound known as Whaleback, found covered by vegetation on the east side of the Damariscotta, was a shell mass of forty-five million cubic feet. On the westerly side, where I probed in the site now owned by George Hart, there are five major mounds, none of which has been exhausted in archaeological terms. They are mute monuments to unrecorded history.

The story of man's beginnings in America is a mystery story. He came out of the shadows, most likely from Asia, across the Bering Strait, along the littoral wilderness, over the Canadian Shield—a primordial gypsy, restless, homeless, always hungry. Archaeologists are closer to his trail than they ever have been before. There are signs that he may have been on the glacier-free slopes of Brooks Range, Alaska, as long as 30,000 years ago. He had traveled as far as Patagonia in 10,000 B.C. He killed bison in the southwest and moved northward and eastward; his route can be traced, generally on high ground, by faint trails of pre-historic flints along the Ohio, Allegheny, Susquehanna, Delaware, Hudson, and Connecticut rivers. Yet the mystery continues. When did he first arrive? If he came from Asia as we believe, how many migrations were there? How many routes were followed? When and where did New World civilization begin?

We have just begun to cross the threshold of discovery. Every spade put into the ground with care helps. Every carefully recorded excavation serves to confirm a standing opinion, or to postulate a new one. In every one of the continental states there are clues to be uncovered, questioned, and finally fitted into their proper places in the enormous unsolved puzzle. When will the key piece be found?

10

Dig It Yourself

I HAVE NO THEORIES about what makes people want to dig. The least complicated answer, I'm sure, must lie in man's innate curiosity, his urge to find out more about himself and his predecessors, his need to know who passed this way before, who stayed to live and how he prospered.

Perhaps too often, digging is irreparably casual and irresponsible; but there are also cautious amateur diggers who are moved to explore the earth solely because of a romantic interest in the past. Sigurd Olson, president of the National Parks Association, has written in *Listening Point* of just such an impulse:

"The diary of Alexander Mackenzie tells of a trading post near Prairie Portage on Basswood Lake [on the Minnesota-Canada border]. I visited that site not long ago, and as we fought the waves across Inlet Bay, I thought of the voyageurs who had come that way and how welcome a sight that post must have been to bush-weary travelers of the past. What a thrill for them to see the beached canoes and the flag flying over the fort, and how they sang as they thought of friends and warmth and rest. That trading post had been a landmark in the lives of many men.

"We went ashore and explored the site, but all we could see was the line of demarcation where the timber stopped, where the pines had been cut to make room for buildings that had stood there. Now the site was grown thickly with hazel and maple, poplar and birch, alder and diamond willow, and we had to hunt to find the telltale mounds and outlines of the foundations. We cut some stakes and began to dig in a corner of one of the buildings and there made our first discoveries, square-headed nails fashioned at forges almost two hundred years ago, bits of clay mortar, bones of deer and moose, turtles and fish, a flint skin-scraper and a pipe stem—enough to know that men had lived there many years."

Abandoned sites where men have lived are abundant, yet very few of them will ever be scientifically explored. Part of the trouble is that there are not enough trained diggers to meet the growing demands on archaeology. Indeed, few archaeologists have any experience at all in the historic sites field, and none has had academic training designed to prepare him for projects in local history. Archaeology is usually taught as a branch of anthropology, with the emphasis on prehistory; or in some universities it may be among courses in the art or classical languages departments. But there are no courses available for one who is moved to devote himself to the long-buried beginnings of white settlements in America. The specialized techniques needed at historic sites can be perfected only through field work.

There are, of course, some basic approaches. To begin, a digger must learn to read the layers of earth through which he cuts as if they were the pages of a book. Stratigraphy, the arrangement of soil strata, is the beginning of accurate interpretation of all that lies buried. Normally the strata are differentiated by variations in color, or substance, or content. A city gardener need only cut into his backyard to discover the stratifications of twentieth-century real estate: he may find a tidy, economical layer of turf, supported by a layer of sand under which may lie a vast accumulation of ashes, tin cans, and other refuse dumped in as fill; beneath these strata he might even find the swamp that had been filled in so that houses could be put up on the land. Recognition of archaeological strata is at once as deceptively simple as this and immeasurably more complex. The buried book of pages must be interpreted with a skill that the amateur can acquire only after long and intense experience.

On page 104 is a section showing the strata found at Philipsburg Manor. Historical research had told us that there had been at least seven occupations of the site, that the contour of the riparian terrain had been deliberately changed on at least three occasions. The task, therefore, was not to dig blithely until we exposed the lower and earliest surface, but to carefully test-trench so that we could examine and record the condition of each stratum and to date the artifacts found. Once we had the story told by the strata, we could use mechanical equipment to make quick work of the fills deposited here since 1683.

There are many instances, like my dig in the Walden woods, where the opportunity for stratigraphic observation is absent, but more often than not the digger must be constantly aware of the layers of earth through which he trenches. He must constantly challenge his findings, for it is all too easy to misinterpret the evidence. When New Jersey state officials asked me to help locate the site of the Batsto ironworks on the Wharton Tract, it developed that previous explorers had come to what seemed the reasonable conclusion that a massive layer of iron slag was evidence of the location of the blast furnace. Their assumption proved to be wrong. Beneath this slaggy stratum—which my test pits showed to be from seven to twelve feet thick—I found a swamp that had been used simply as a dump for the ironworks refuse. The actual site of the works was yards away on higher ground; there trenching revealed strata bearing iron artifacts still lying on the working-surfaces.

The beginnings of accurate interpretation, however, come long before the shovel bites the dirt. I cannot stress enough the need to gather and assimilate every scrap of information relative to the projected dig. The digger must examine the written record of the activity at the site, of the products made or utensils used, of the people and their habits. I frequently go beyond the archives, and interview elderly residents who, though their memories may not always be as accurate as they think, can contribute impressions carried over from childhood that are surprisingly valuable. Experience proves that seldom, if ever, is enough documentary material assembled in advance of excavation. But the compilation of this material reduces the chance that underground clues will be misinterpreted.

How do archaeologists know where to dig? James B. Pritchard, who in 1956 found the Biblical city of Gibeon eight feet below a Jordanian tomato farm, selected his site "on the theory that the ancient city must have been on the brow of the hump nearest the main spring." He reasoned that an abundant water source must be a central factor in the growth of any settlement, and in three days of digging he cut into a tunnel that led him from the spring to Gibeon's buried town square; the passage carved through hard limestone with primitive tools had been built to prevent the possibility of any enemy cutting off the ancient city from its water supply.

Pritchard's correct deduction of the close relationship of the spring to the Gibeon townsite can be applied to the pursuit of any lost settlement. And, in America, the early towns needed water not only to drink but as a source of power, to run the sawmills, the grist mills, to turn the wheels that moved the bellows fanning the first forges. The shores of America's moving streams are replete with archaeological remains.

But let's attack a tougher problem. In the first half of the nineteenth century a townsite was staked out on the bluff above a Minnesota river. The state historian tells us that a wishful city-founder built cabins of round tamarack logs, daubed with clay instead of mortar. He tells us of a pioneer who remembered that the clay didn't stick well but fell out in the wind and rain. "Three times that year," the pioneer recalled, "she froze her feet, and coffee froze in cups while the family was sitting at the table. Their monotonous diet lacked salt, potatoes, eggs, milk, and most other necessities, yet they managed to survive. They may even have enjoyed life a little, for she remembered that on the first Christmas they served dinner to all the Indians in a camp nearby." The historian records that the struggling settlement had a courthouse with a basement, and back of this the founder put up a building of stone. Not surprisingly, considering the privations, this dream of a boom city in the Middle West faded. The enterprising founder finally gave up in disgust, his structures were left to ruin, and years later a second settlement began to prosper a short distance to the south.

With no other facts than these, the ill-fated town can be found. In the historian's account the archaeologist would be struck first by the courthouse with a basement. On the small farms that exist today north of the present settlement, he would put little faith in the chance of finding Indian artifacts in sufficient quantity to lead him to the "camp nearby" of those who had come to Christmas dinner. Constant plowing eliminates too much in the way of sur-

Dig It Yourself

face relics; plowing also would reduce the possibility of finding the footings of the stone house. But the basement foundation must still be evident. How first to locate the spot to dig? Any settlers along a river would have had continual traffic to the water's edge. Patient and exhaustive examination of the bluff north of the second settlement—combing through the twentieth-century vegetation with a perceptive eye—will turn up signs of a foot path, perhaps even a wagon trail over which meager supplies had been carried upward from boats. Even though grassed over, a hillside path can still be recognized as an obscure impression in the earth. That impression can be followed to the summit and to the general area in which the makers of the path once lived. Still the archaeologist is far from having pinpointed his target—the buried remains of the cellar—for we can assume that at the end of the path the soil has been cultivated. As he examines the level land, the scientific digger looks sharply for even the slightest settling of earth, for he knows that if the cellar hole has been filled in, the fill will require scores of years before it becomes as tightly packed as soil undisturbed by man. After holes are filled and leveled the fill gradually sinks, leaving a slight depression which can be observed by the trained eye. In a dry summer the grass withers more quickly where the earth is shallow over stone foundations.

But no digger should break out his shovel at first recognition of such a minute depression. Without digging, he can make sure he has not been misled by sinking his probe rod along the edges of the depression in search of cellar walls. My probe rods, the first of which I had made when I was teaching myself the fundamentals at Walden, are the most exercised of my tools. They are made of steel, five-eighths of an inch in diameter, with a T-bar handle at one end, a sharp tapered point at the other, and they vary in length from four to six feet.

The general technique is to grip the handle with two hands and

plunge the rod into the earth in one motion. The secret now is not
to exert strength, but to widen the puncture in the ground by
reaming. I've had at least a dozen workers who could not understand this. Instead of reaming, they insisted upon only a downward
pressure, or on bending the rod sideways. But properly done, the
technique of plunging and reaming will carry the rod its full length

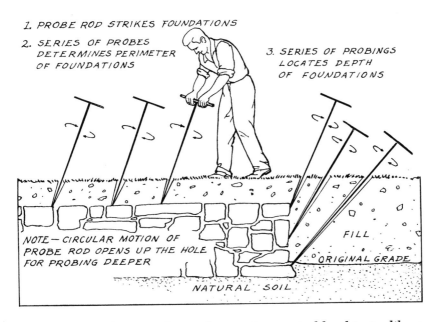

1. PROBE ROD STRIKES FOUNDATIONS

2. SERIES OF PROBES
   DETERMINES PERIMETER
   OF FOUNDATIONS

3. SERIES OF PROBINGS
   LOCATES DEPTH
   OF FOUNDATIONS

NOTE— CIRCULAR MOTION OF
PROBE ROD OPENS UP THE HOLE
FOR PROBING DEEPER

FILL

ORIGINAL GRADE

NATURAL SOIL

into the ground, or until it strikes an impenetrable object—like a
stone wall. The rod makes fill soils instantly recognizable because
it sinks through them so much more easily than through Nature's
eons-old strata. It takes persistent reaming to penetrate natural
layers of clay. And a stratum of hardpan, to cite a specific example,
will feel as hard, when the rod first strikes it, as stone. Hitting a
stone underground for the first time is an experience. Once the rod
has reamed an opening, the user begins to put his weight into
driving the point deeper and deeper. When he hits a boulder, the
boulder doesn't give one iota. The shock trembles in the rod, runs

Dig It Yourself

through the hands and on up to the shoulders. When the digger takes his hands from the rod he finds them shaking, just as if he had been suddenly charged with electricity.

As the rod is forced down toward the boulder, however, it may go through a stratum of sand; this will seem mealy to the prober. When my rod strikes gravel, as if often does, I'm reminded of nothing so much as a collection of marbles in a sand box. Buried wood gives off the sound of an underground thud when the point bites in and sticks, and the sensation has seemed almost identical when I have struck a hard-packed earthen floor covered with layers of fill.

But let's return to the hypothetical archaeologist we left surveying the possible site of a cellar in the ill-fated Minnesota town. Probing along the edge of the depression, he strikes stone. To determine whether it is a natural boulder or part of a wall, the next step is to plunge the rod down a few inches away from his first trial. If he again strikes stone at the same level, he probes a little farther from the original point, as many times as necessary to strike the edge of the stone. If what he has found is actually a wall, he can trace each side of it by careful probing, as well as getting an idea of the depth to which it penetrates. Having determined its width, further probing will outline the directions in which the wall runs and will tell when a corner is reached and which way the adjoining wall runs. The archaeologist hunting a cellar of a ruined courthouse in a lost Minnesota settlement can locate the foundation and accurately describe its dimensions before he ever touches a shovel. With this accomplished he can dig if he chooses.

In the study of prehistory in America, identification of a site may be as easy as recognizing a large mound composed of discarded clam shells, or it may only become possible when buried arrow points and pottery fragments are turned up by the annual plowing of a field. The difference is that the mound reveals a more or less permanent village and the scattered artifacts may indicate only a camp at which a migrant group might have stopped for a brief period. Sites are often identified "collectively"—when archaeological amateurs co-operate by pooling the artifacts and clues they have found. When there is little but local legend to point to a site, the experienced archaeologist puts off digging until he has explored the deeds and all the various records which may contain references to the area. Thus armed, his next step is to inspect every inch of ground—a survey job in which two men might cover as much as five square miles a day. Even when there are no obvious manifestations such as a funeral mound thrusting out of the plane or an earthen fort camouflaged by vegetation, he may still have success. Like Sir Leonard Woolley, he may take advantage of a rise of ground and a peculiar slanting of the sun's rays to see clues absolutely invisible on the surface.

"One evening," Sir Leonard says in *Digging Up the Past*, "we climbed a little hill . . . to watch the sunset over the Nile; we were grumbling over our ill luck when suddenly MacIver pointed to the plane at our feet; its whole surface was dotted with dark circles which, though we tramped over it day after day, we had never seen. I ran down the hill and the circles vanished as I came close to them but, guided by MacIver from above, I made little piles of gravel here and there, one in the middle of each ring; and when we started digging there next morning our Arab workmen found under each pile the square, rock-cut shaft of a tomb. . . . 4,000 years had produced a dead level of stone and gravel where the eye could distinguish no difference of arrangement or texture. . . . The sun's rays, coming at a particular angle, brought out a darker tint to be seen only from above, and perhaps from a single point."

Long-established Indian village sites are much more easily recognized because of their substantial size and because of the presence of a midden—the community refuse heap—that is usually

Dig It Yourself

fairly deep. Midden soil is more often than not recognizable almost immediately because it is darker than the natural soil around it, and may be greasy in texture as the result of decomposition of animal and vegetable matter. The deeper color is the result of ash and charcoal, the latter being particularly resistant to decay.

Indian campsites are characterized by thin middens, usually close to the surface; they represent the occupation for a limited time of a small number of people, such as a hunting party, and though the artifacts found will be no less valuable they will be fewer in number.

In general practice, sites are most often found through surface artifacts, all of which are retained no matter how unimportant they may seem. One trick, used by Middle Westerners while searching over the ground, is to watch out for miniscule colored beads in the traffic lanes of anthills; often an industrious ant worker returns from burrowing in an Indian grave with a sparkling cargo removed from a necklace or a disintegrated buckskin jacket. A veteran anthropologist at the University of South Dakota used to float down the Missouri on a raft, scanning the shore as if he were an Indian real estate expert. When he spotted a place that seemed likely for building a village he would go ashore and run a test trench. More often than not he found the kind of remains he was seeking. Similarly, it was the deposit of brick fragments along a path that eventually led me to find the right spot in which to dig at Walden.

It is only when a site is located and its history thoroughly studied that the real work begins. If a site is overgrown with brush and trees it must be cleared to facilitate the search for any possible surface artifacts. Where there are no clues above ground but where the general area of a buried structure has been located, the technique of test-trenching is necessary to gain quick knowledge of stratigraphy. Then plans for further digging can be made.

Amateurs digging under supervision at Crown Point, New York, have unearthed many relics of early eighteenth-century life.

Planning is the essential. While there may be an element of luck in any dig, it doesn't follow that scientific excavation is pure gamble. It is the archaeologist who thinks out every recognizable phase of his problem *before* he digs who eliminates unnecessary work and achieves his goal soonest. He makes his plans on the basis of research and a common-sense study of existing conditions at the site. He locates his site precisely on an accurate map of the general area, photographs it as it appears before excavation begins, and keeps a record of the stratigraphy and the relative location of artifacts.

It is often important to draw a detailed map of the site itself. Reference to streets should be established in urban problems, and such features as slopes, streams, beaches, paths, fences, and trees

Dig It Yourself

should be included wherever pertinent. Every test pit or trench must be specifically located on the site map.

Much the simplest form of diagraming the location of an excavation is called triangulation. Established landmarks are used as fixed points, and the location is made by measuring the distance from two such fixed points to all the corners of the excavation. Thus, even though the hole is completely filled in, it can be relocated speedily.

As in my Jefferson dig at Shadwell, there are numerous occasions when a grid pattern should be imposed over the site. The digger begins by arbitrarily establishing well outside the dimensions of the site a zero point, or datum, at which he drives in a stake similar to a surveyor's monument. From this stake, running north and east, he lays out a network of squares of convenient size, say five feet. At each corner he drives in a stake that he clearly labels A1, A2, B1, B2, etc., the numbers running north and south and the letters east and west. In this way he excavates one square at a time and is able to keep a specific record of stratigraphical variations and the exact horizontal and vertical location of artifacts. To accurately record vertical locations, an arbitrary height of 100'00" can be assigned to the ground level at the base of the stake at the datum point. By using a line level the tops of all the stakes in the grid pattern are then made level with datum. Variations in terrain are marked on each stake: if the ground level at A3 is two inches higher than at datum, stake A3 is marked 100'2"— and A4 may accordingly be marked 100'2.5", if the ground is rising. The elevation of various strata and the vertical positions of artifacts are measured in reference to the arbitrary level.

The most common method of excavating squares is to dig one at a time, using a shovel to remove the earth in six-inch layers, or in layers defined by the coloration of the strata. In this way it is almost impossible to fail to observe and accurately measure the

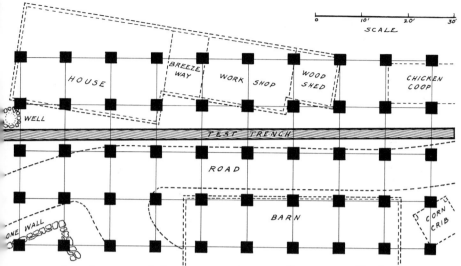

The advantage of digging test pits according to a grid plan instead of using a continuous trench is clearly shown in this hypothetical map of a farm site. The shaded bar represents a trench one hundred feet long and two feet wide which fails to reveal any of the buried foundations. Exactly the same amount of digging is represented by fifty two-foot square test pits, shown here in black. Distributed on a ten-foot grid pattern they cut into each of the farm structures.

depth of pertinent data. Each shovelful may be screened to insure against loss of relics, and when a rich deposit, fertile with artifacts, is come upon, the shovel must be abandoned for a trowel or putty knife.

There is much to be said about artifacts—and some of it will be said in another chapter—but it is important to point out here that the beginning digger can't be too cautious in his interpretation of anything he finds. Digging into the cellar foundation in that lost Minnesota settlement, our hypothetical archaeologist might have found an 1837 American penny just below the bite of the plowshare. This would be meaningless, for the coin might have been dropped at any time and buried when the cellar was filled. Artifacts become valuable in dating historic sites when they are found on contact surfaces—as on the floors used by the earliest occupants.

As he digs down into a cellar hole, the careful excavator will first establish a grid pattern on the surface. He then may find that under the top soil there is a deep stratum of pure junk. It may be that the site was used as pasture and the farmer filled the cavity to protect his animals from falling in and breaking their valuable legs; he dumped everything and anything into it—rubbish, furnace ashes, broken tools, worn-out furniture, boulders by the ton. Beneath this gallimaufry of fill is where the pay dirt lies, and where caution is imperative.

If the structure above the cellar burned, the digger may be in luck. Among the wood ashes he may find charred beams that supported a second story. He may find the burned remains of bedroom furnishings lying on top of the beams, and below the beams some cooking utensils. If he finds enough of such artifacts to form a pattern, he may be able to begin reconstructing the general arrangement of the building—at one end the early occupants had had their kitchen, and over it a bedroom. The charred spine of a leather-bound book and a fragment of a gilt picture frame might help conjecturally to locate the parlor. But most important of all would be his search for a chimney base; wherever there is habitation there has to be at the very least a hearth.

Instead of destruction by fire, let's assume for the moment that our building was dismantled by someone wanting sawed lumber with which to build in another place. Let's assume, too, that the cellar was carved out of natural clay and that it never was buttressed by a foundation wall. Again the chance of finding it is good, and again the probe rod can be of help. As the excavator goes over the depression that is the telltale sign of an area containing fill soils, the rod which goes down with some ease in the center of the depression will "react" when it is used outside the depression: If the natural clay lies, say, eight inches below the surface, the plunge of the rod will be slowed down when it strikes this buried stratum. Maneuvering as carefully as he did to find the edges of the foundation stones, the prober can now locate the sides of the cellar that were cut into clay. Excavation proceeds in the usual way even though the lack of fire evidence eliminates the probability of significant artifacts in any abundance. Only objects found on the hard-packed cellar floor—the contact surface—can be assumed to be of value, and these only when they can be associated chronologically with the known period of occupation.

Of a number of digging methods used at Indian sites, the commonest is known as the Unit-Level Method. Using either a trowel or a shovel, the excavator removes a layer of soil from the surface of a single square. Any artifacts found during this operation are placed in a bag and marked. The new surface is leveled off and cleaned of all loose dirt before the second layer is removed. Again any artifacts found are bagged and marked, and the processes are repeated until sterile soil—devoid of artifacts—is reached. The difference between the dark midden soil, in which relics appear, and the generally much lighter subsoil is usually so obvious that the digger should have no question about the point at which he reaches bottom. But, to be absolutely sure, most diggers cut into the subsoil to a depth of at least six inches on the chance of locating early burials. In my own work, I go much deeper, for soils can be deceptive, even to one with much experience.

The accumulation of artifacts can sometimes be the only means of locating a vanished structure. In the Shadwell dig I was unable to define the four corners of the house not only because the house had been leveled, but because it had never had a full-scale cellar and the foundations for the walls had been scattered by the plow. Yet as I excavated the ten-foot grid squares, uncovering thousands

Dig It Yourself

of eighteenth-century brick fragments and handmade nails, a pattern of concentration began to develop. It began to be apparent that so great an accumulation of building materials, all within a limited area, indicated the site of the house destroyed by fire; ashes, charcoal, and other relics showing evidence of fire followed the same pattern. To preserve this concentration of evidence I recorded the number of brick pieces, then sorted the other associated objects, and put the accumulation of each grid square into a large paper bag which was marked with the date of excavation, the designation of the square, and the bag's contents.

Artifacts are seldom as impersonal as the remnants of a burned building. More often, they are objects more closely related to human beings. Archaeologists are frequently accused of being too fond of digging up the dead, even though it must be obvious that important kinds of information come from graves. Prehistoric skeletons tell us much about the kind of people who lived in unrecorded times and places, and man-made objects help us to picture the mode of life, the religious and social habits that make one civilization different from another.

Sir Mortimer Wheeler, in his *Archaeology from the Earth*, has some well chosen words on the subject. He says: "The variety of burial-ritual devised by man in his care alike for the departed and for their survivors are legion. The body may be buried intact or after cremation; it may be left awhile to the weather, the kites, and the jackals, whereafter a few representative bones may be collected and piously interred. Burials may be communal or individual. The dead may be thrust with no durable equipment into the earth; they may be accompanied by the treasury of Sutton Hoo; or by a sumptuous army of attendants as at Ur; they may go naked to St. Peter or with a harem to Paradise; they may be enclosed in a humble pot or in relays of costly sarcophagi; their grave may be marked by no lasting monument or by 'a mound on a hill, high and broad, by wave-farers wide to be seen'; or their ashes may be tipped into a river which will bear them happily from our ken. Fear, habit, a little affection, and much affectation go to the making of these things. It is fortunate for the prying archaeologist that his technical problem is often a relatively simple one. His difficulty begins when he comes to reconstruct the ritual represented by the particles of evidence uncovered by his skill; and if he steps beyond ritual to its fanciful significance, he will scarcely find the answer. . . ."

Human skeletons call for even more than the usual caution. Experienced diggers try first to determine the position of the burial, ascertaining whether the interment was in the flexed position common among prehistoric peoples or whether the skeleton is horizontally extended. Because the skull is usually highest, it is most often discovered first in stripping operations and is the signal for tentative digging with trowel or putty knife. Key parts —elbows, pelvis, and knees—are thus located, as are what funerary artifacts there may be. Some archaeologists prefer to leave the bones partially embedded and to excavate an entire slab of earth without disturbing the position of the skeletal parts.

Many diggers, much to their embarrassment, have learned that there are laws against disturbing the dead—and these can be applied even to burials made long before man taught himself to write. The discovery of human bones always awakens local interest and rarely can be kept quiet. The sooner the archaeologist reports such a find to the coroner or the state police the less apt he is to have to do some fast explaining—for the law has a way of jumping at conclusions.

For instance, in 1955 when Asa Johnston, an Iowa sand and gravel man, found some bones in the scoop of his bulldozer, he trotted to the coroner's office and helped piece together a skeleton on the office couch. It seemed for a moment that the mystery had been lifted in the case of a local man who had disappeared fifteen years before. It was on second thought—when the bones began to disintegrate in the air-conditioned office—that the coroner called in a paleontologist. Suddenly Johnston's gravel pit seemed to fill up with scientists, and the task force soon found three more complete human skeletons, along with most of the bones of a prehistoric bison. The stratum in which they were found set the date of burial at about 7000 B.C.

No coroner was consulted when Keith Glasscock unearthed a broken skull on the Scharbauer ranch near Midland, Texas. Glasscock had no doubt he had made a prehistoric find, and he went directly to Dr. Fred Wendorf of the New Mexico Laboratory of Anthropology. In what has been called in academic language "an excellent example of interdisciplinary cooperation in archaeological research," Wendorf enlisted the help of Dr. Alex Krieger, Dr. T. Dale Stewart, Dr. F. J. McLure and Dr. Claude C. Albritton. Thus combining the resources of paleontology, archaeology, geology, physical anthropology, and dentistry, the experts submitted the skull fragments to months of study and determined that they were contemporary with other bones of a number of now extinct animals which were unearthed through Glasscock's find at the same prehistoric waterhole.

Few sites can be expected to be so rewarding, yet skeletal remains should always be carefully studied. They should be photographed just as they are found—before removal—and each separate piece should be placed in its own bag and labeled.

I have pointed out that archaeologists in America are under pressure to salvage as much as possible from sites threatened by destruction through natural causes such as erosion, or by construction operations such as the building of dams or roads. No urgency is attached to the more leisurely excavations which fall into the category of problem-solving, the kind of digging that has occupied so many of my friends in the Massachusetts Archaeological Society. These men are dedicated to learning all they can of prehistoric life in the state. One group, for example, has spent a half-dozen years studying a small valley on Cape Cod, and has built up a detailed picture of two distinct hunting and food-gathering cultures which thrived here in the pre-Christian era. As is true of their counterparts in other states, their careful, published reports add considerably to our common store of knowledge about the past.

Such reports obviously are only as good as the field records upon which they are based. Field notes are best kept in a bound book so that there is no chance of losing pages. Each page should be headed with the date and the site designation. With approach to excavation, the site should be described as it appears and the manner of excavation outlined. Stratifications must be measured as they are uncovered, and described exactly in the notebook. If the layers meet, interlock, or overlap in the section opened, this condition should be not only described but illustrated with a measured sketch.

Notes about artifacts cannot be too detailed, if the object is pertinent to occupation, for it is this information that often goes far toward positively dating the occupation. No pertinent object should be removed from the soil before it has been photographed and its position described in the notebook; its position should be measured exactly, in both horizontal and vertical directions, and a note made of its distance from any associated relic.

Digging alone is worthless, for digging is destruction. It is this recording of all the facets of careful observation that separates the digger with a sense of historical responsibility from the "pot hunter." It has been said that "it is not what you find, but how you find it that counts," and the "how" becomes useful only when it is accurately and completely set down in notes. Only proper records

Dig It Yourself

that include all the details of geographical and human influences can make excavation valid. Without such records, meticulously kept, no digging, no matter how earnest, can be of interest to science—it is like a history in which all dates have been omitted.

Still this isn't the end of it. When the excavation is completed, the notebook filled, the artifacts recorded and catalogued, there are two important though sometimes tedious jobs remaining. Even if a digger owns the property on which he has worked, there will be few occasions when he will be justified in leaving his pits open— for even archaeological excavations can be dangerous. Backfilling is important. The grade should be restored and the turf returned so that the site is left in reasonable semblance of the way it was found.

To equip oneself for active archaeology there are a number of tools which are essential to success.

FIELD EQUIPMENT

The basic items for a survey include:

Probe rod
Army trench shovel
Putty knife or trowel
Camera
Compass
Rolled-steel pocket tape measure, and 100′ tape
Graph paper for mapping
File cards for descriptions of finds
Bound notebook for photographs and field observations
Waterproof paper bags
First-aid kit

For a full-scale excavation, the tools may vary with the condition of the site. The following list is a minimum for a single digger:

Probe rod

Some of the tools used on a full-scale excavation. The satchel at the right contains putty knives, trowels, and other small items.

Spade-pointed excavating-shovel
8-inch putty knife
Four to six inch pointing-trowel
100′ rolled steel tape
U.S. Army Engineers pocket compass
One-inch and two-inch paint brushes, whisk broom, scrub brush
Portable screen for sifting earth
Bound notebooks
File cards
Mapping-paper
Waterproof bags and cardboard boxes
First-aid kit

Dig It Yourself

IN ADDITION, THERE SHOULD BE AVAILABLE AT THE SITE:
Picks and mattocks
Shaker screens
Water buckets
Wheelbarrow
Hatchets or clippers for removing roots
Carpenter's level, engineer's line level, and cord
Waterproof marking-devices (Magic Marker)
Canvas or tarpaper for protecting turf from dumped soil
Cameras and photographic equipment
Ladders

AND FOR THE PRESERVATION OF DETERIORATING ARTIFACTS:
White shellac in alcohol
Benzine and beeswax
Alvar
Krylon
Duco cement
Soft tissues
Brushes and sprayers

11

Underground Photography

As I write this, it is estimated that fifty million Americans are out taking pictures at the rate of sixty-seven hundred snaps a minute. With this in mind, it is difficult to imagine anyone interested in archaeological digging who would not be equipped to make his own photographs.

Yet we are in a field in which something more is required than equipment and enthusiasm, for archaeology demands pictures that are accurate rather than pretty or amusing. The camera becomes an instrument to be used as relentlessly as a lie detector; it must be trained to tell the truth. Because photographs are so important a part of the archaeologist's record, they must report, without distortion, every step in the progress of the excavation.

The digger almost never knows exactly what he is going to find underground and usually the finds cover more territory than is expected. Therefore it is imperative to shoot the area from all angles, picturing the shape and elevation of the site itself, as well as the streams, the vegetation, and the contours of the adjoining countryside; shots from as many points of the compass as possible should be made at a distance of about a hundred yards. As much as I have photographed my various projects, as many individual pictures as I have made at each site, I have never made enough. Something always turns up before the dig is finished to make me wish that I had not neglected some specific angle.

For instance, many digs eventually spread out over as much area as the one at Saugus. There, though we located the blast furnace at once, we didn't know there was the site of a water wheel under Central Street. To make the record complete, to show the contrast between the seventeenth- and twentieth-century contours, we needed panoramic pictures made before any excavations began. Of course we took many such pictures; personally I took over three thousand color transparencies and five thousand feet of 16mm color movies; our photographer took more than one thousand black-and-white pictures, and we had several dozen aerial photographs taken. Yet there was often a certain angle or detail which I neglected to photograph—and which could never be photographed because our work had altered the scene.

Even pictures made at a distance of one hundred yards must be sharp in minute details to be of value. They should be taken at various times during the day, under various light conditions, in order to use shadow as emphasis in some cases, or to eliminate it altogether in others. A near-by hill, a treetop, or even the top of a station wagon frequently will provide the elevation to make pictures more effective. And sometimes, because of light factors similar to those which helped Sir Leonard Woolley to spot the graves beside the Nile, the camera will pick up clues which are invisible to the eye alone.

Photographs taken from airplanes are especially effective. For sunken structures leave permanent traces on the surface of the land which are obscure when viewed at eye level. Buried walls tend to stunt root growth, while tunnels give roots additional room and thus produce more luxuriant crops. Seen from the sky this varied vegetal condition will clearly outline what lies buried. Archaeologists hunting the site of a Roman town at Silchester, England, found that aerial photographs showed clear demarcations of streets buried for fifteen hundred years, even though the present surface was criss-crossed by thick hedgerows and modern roads.

A more unusual method has lately been developed by an Italian amateur archaeologist named Carlo Lerici who makes photographs *beneath* the existing surface before he starts to excavate. Lerici began by studying aerial maps of that section of the Roman countryside where there are buried Etruscan tombs. Some of them had been robbed of their valuable contents many centuries ago, but some still retained priceless objects. As he expected, the photos taken from the air revealed dim circles indicating the location of the tombs.

To determine the presence or absence of grave furnishings without wholesale excavation, Lerici evolved a unique approach. He marked off the area in twelve-foot grids, driving in metal stakes to which he joined a weak electric current, thus measuring the electrical resistance in the soil. Wherever there was a tomb, its underground air space increased the resistance and signaled to Lerici the tomb's approximate dimensions. In the next step in his new method, Lerici sinks holes just large enough to accommodate a tiny camera and synchronized flash attached to an aluminum tube. Snapping the shutter above ground, he turns the camera to photograph the tomb interior at numerous angles.

In one ten week period, he photographed one hundred and

thirty graves and opened the best twenty of them. The reward included two hundred specimens of ancient pottery and the skeletons of two affluent Etruscans.

Yet such imaginative equipment is far from necessary in the average dig. I still use the camera I bought to replace one which strayed away from me at Walden. Stopping for lunch one day, I hid the camera, a jacknife, and a number of interesting artifacts beside one of Thoreau's trees and, eating a sandwich as I walked, I began to inspect a near-by area. When I returned, though the valuable relics were still there, camera and jacknife were gone. I had to drive over to a Concord drug store to buy the 40-millimeter Bantam which has served me so well.

My practice has been to shoot color transparencies, and to have any I need for publication copied in black and white. I also use a Polaroid Land camera that makes a black-and-white transparency I can project on a screen minutes after it is taken. This is very useful in studying a field problem, and when I am lecturing, it takes my audience into the field and explains the work we were doing only hours earlier. There is no reason to dream of exotic equipment and top-level facilities. I make no claims to being an expert photographer, but I made myself familiar with my Bantam by reading over and over again the instruction pamphlet which came with it. The thousands of pictures which have resulted from that study are proof enough to me that one needs nothing more than mastery of basic techniques and an understanding of the simplest of cameras. Rather than use a light meter, I depend entirely on the standard cardboard radial guides which give instructions for focal apertures under any light conditions one is apt to encounter. It is a simple system which has never failed.

Undoubtedly it must seem too simple. No well organized academic expedition would think of appearing in the field without a giant plate camera with at least three types of lenses, a small hand camera, filters galore, tripods, and a mobile tower as dashing as a Hollywood movie-maker's boom. Between this extreme and my own practice there is the comfortable medium of many amateurs who use a camera with a minimum negative size of 2¼ x 2¼ inches and a lens speed of ƒ6.3 or faster. With tripod, flash-bulb attachment, and a set of three filters they are well equipped for field photography. Red filters are particularly useful in delineating the difference between reddish and blackish soils in stratigraphic pictures. Yellow produces tone values closer to those seen by the naked eye, and green will come in handy when it is important to emphasize red and black tones.

Every archaeological picture needs a scale—either a person caught in some reasonable act (nothing is worse than a model looking like a self-conscious statue) or a graduated rule. Because yardsticks and tape measures have figures so small that reading is difficult in a photograph, I've devised a giant tape which is simple to make and easy to carry. Out of yellow poster-board bought at a stationery or art store, I cut four-inch strips which I staple or glue together to make a six-foot length. Measuring off feet and inches, I paint black figures from one to six, as large as possible, with a lettering device known as a Magic-Marker. This home-made measure rolls neatly away when it is not in use, and shows very clearly in photographs when it is used to scale anything from the depth of a trench to the length of a water-wheel spoke. The yellow paper does not reflect the sun's glare but does stand out against any background.

An identification marker should also be set up to be included in the photograph. If, for instance, the picture is to show a trench dug in section A3 of a grid pattern, this designation should be printed on a card and propped up so that it can be seen plainly when the photograph is printed; when a card is not at hand, the simplest thing is to print the designation on a page of the field

Underground Photography

notebook, spreading its covers so that it will stand by itself. When artifacts are photographed *in situ*, they should also be labeled plainly for the camera, a card being attached to the wall of the trench by a nail or a small peg.

In photographing artifacts after they have been cleaned and treated to insure their preservation, it is most desirable to photograph them against a perfectly shadowless background. It is sometimes convenient to place the object on the floor or on a low table, the camera being mounted on a swivel-socket tripod and tipped with the lens directly down. To make the artifact stand out clearly, it is frequently placed on a white matte-finished cardboard, or on black velvet if its value and coloration may be thus enhanced. Let's assume, though that an antique pistol has been unearthed, restored and is ready for a portrait. With any such article that combines dull surfaces such as bone or wood with reflective metal the best method is to place a sheet of light cardboard on the floor, and over it, supported by wooden blocks about eight inches high, place a pane of plate glass. The pistol is put on the center of the glass and the camera focused directly over it. Lights should then be placed so that shadows are out of the camera's view.

Every frame of exposed film, whether made in the field or at the time of processing the artifacts, must be recorded in a special notebook. Date and hour of the shooting is put down, along with the frame number, the atmospheric conditions, the artificial light used, and a full description of the subject. The same information is filed with the black-and-white negative or the transparency, as the case may be.

The camera's value cannot be overestimated. It preserves a record of the destruction that is a necessary part of any excavation. Frequently the image it records is all that remains of a disintegrating vestige of past life. It is a tool to be used wisely—one that never can be used too often.

12

Pipe Hunting, Potsherds, Arrowheads, and Artifacts

Giovanni Belzoni, who began as a nineteenth-century strong man in a London circus, may well have been the greatest archaeological collector the world has known, but his scorn for scientific methods is notorious. In becoming an Egyptian explorer he could not restrain his muscular talent. He was a plunderer, so eager to acquire antiquities that he smashed tombs open in the Valley of the Kings, and used every vandalistic trick he could think of to add new buried treasures to museum collections.

In his restless, ruthless urge to acquire he was a swashbuckling giant who set an example that crossed the Atlantic and poisoned nineteenth-century Americans by the hundreds. "Pot-hunting"—still a dirty word to responsible archaeologists—became a pastime in this country. Traveling shows at the turn of the century made fortunes displaying Indian objects; they were eager to buy whatever relic a mining prospector or a cowboy might dig up in the southwest. Fashionable housewives developed romantic notions about the Noble Savage, decorating their parlors with Pueblo pots, their persons with shell bead necklaces. Untold quantities of invaluable artifacts were rooted from the soil, their locations unobserved and unrecorded, their scientific value lost in the scourge of looting that had become big business. It was not until professional archaeologists forced through the Antiquities Act in 1906 that controls were established to save the underground record of civilization's development in the United States.

The underground record of white settlement is, obviously, no less valuable. As we have seen, it is a quarter-century since government archaeologists began to dig at Jamestown, and they are still at it, adding more and more relics to the half-million already brought from the earth. These artifacts, broken, rust-encrusted, half disintegrated, led diggers to an unrecorded mass burial, mute evidence of the desperate effort of the Jamestown settlers to keep the Indians ignorant of their losses during the "starving time" of 1609-10. No map or picture of the town survives, yet digging uncovered the remains of picket fences and drainage ditches that served as boundaries. The finding of potsherds located the site of the pottery kiln; the glasshouse was pinpointed when pieces of old

This Jamestown kiln burned oyster shells to produce lime for making glass and other purposes. The iron hoops which supported the arched top of the kiln buckled from the intense heat.

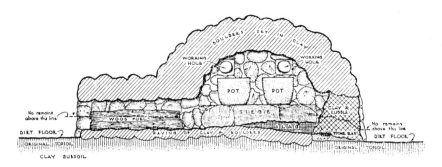

Conjectural reconstruction of main glass furnace found at Jamestown, Virginia.

crucibles turned up, and fragments of household goods led to the
excavation of one hundred and forty structures. Artifacts helped to
decipher the map of Jamestown in the earth. Rust-eaten axes,
wedges, and saws help, also, to illuminate the struggle to clear the
wilderness. We can identify the site of the earliest known British
armorer's forge, and we are far closer to Captain Smith when
we examine a matchlock musket or a siege helmet wrested from
the very soil on which he commanded Jamestown guards.

Colonial artifacts reflect a kinship of purpose. Beside the James
River, along the Delaware, the Hudson, the Connecticut, the same
kinds of relics are found, and they form a hazy trail that tells of
common artisanship, common struggles, similar ventures in commerce. Barter with the Indians had created a demand for almost
anything made of iron, and colonists north and south were busy
trading items like shears, knives, and hatchets for corn, fish, game,
fruits, and furs. Certainly the Ironworks at Saugus had contributed
to this exchange, but we could not know to what degree until we
attempted to interpret the artifacts with accuracy.

The value of these Saugus finds was not simply in telling us
more about the range of activity of the ironworkers; they offered

Pipe Hunting, Potsherds, Arrowheads, Artifacts

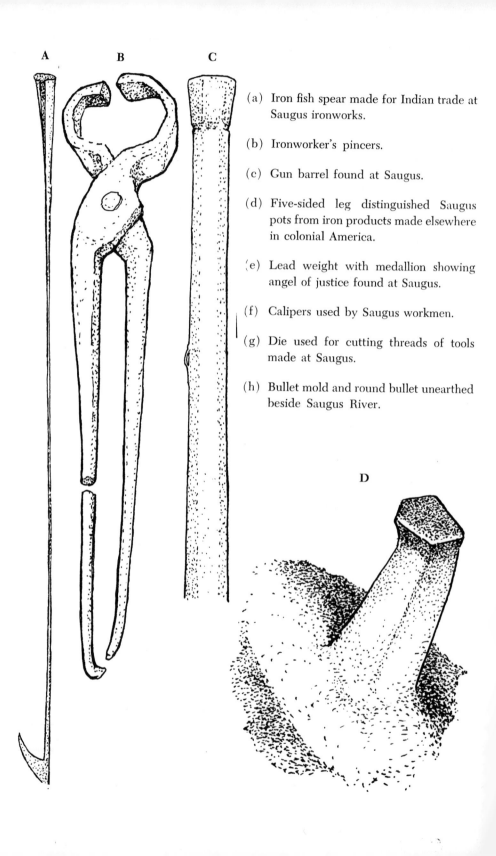

(a) Iron fish spear made for Indian trade at Saugus ironworks.

(b) Ironworker's pincers.

(c) Gun barrel found at Saugus.

(d) Five-sided leg distinguished Saugus pots from iron products made elsewhere in colonial America.

(e) Lead weight with medallion showing angel of justice found at Saugus.

(f) Calipers used by Saugus workmen.

(g) Die used for cutting threads of tools made at Saugus.

(h) Bullet mold and round bullet unearthed beside Saugus River.

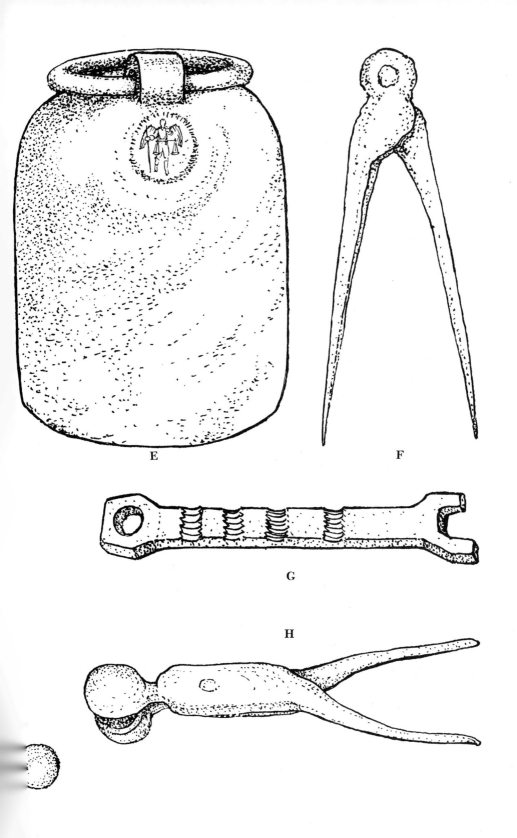

E

F

G

H

opportunity for further study to other specialists. Students of Indian life, especially, were interested in the chance to relate Ironworks artifacts to items of white manufacture found at Indian sites. By assessing these in the light of other projects, such as Jamestown, much can be added to the knowledge of colonial traffic with the Indians. A single excavation almost never offers a record in any way complete, but the collation of interpretations from several digs—the careful comparison of artifacts found in Virginia with those in Massachusetts—the finding of Saugus-manufactured articles in the middens of Indian villages or as funerary offerings in burials—these things make the artifact an incisive tool of history.

As an example of how artifacts are used in this kind of co-operation, I quote the Saugus report of William S. Fowler, curator of the Bronson Museum at Attleboro, Massachusetts:

"Among many objects recovered from the Ironworks, those that seem significant for archaeological comparison as representing articles often used in barter with the Indians are brass spoons, clay pipes, brass pins, jew's-harps, iron fishhooks, and small iron axes or hatchets." Fowler had special interest in the hatchets, particularly after Neal Hartley discovered a letter written by an apprentice of Joseph Jenks, a man named William Curtis, whose toolmaker's die, engraved with his initials, we had unearthed in the damp soil at the Jenks site. In the letter which Fowler cites, Curtis applied in about 1657 for a job with John Winthrop, Jr., who had opened an ironworks in Connecticut. Fowler goes on:

"Curtis puts it quaintly in this way: 'Master John Winthrop, I remember my loving service to you hoping you are in good health as I am at present and I will be your smith, if you please, to make all your iron ware which belongs to forge or furnace, and I know there is none that can do it so well as they that are used to it, and to make all sorts of ware that the Country has need of both for

Englishmen and Indians and I hope to be profitable for you and I rest you as your loving friend.' Here it may be seen that the Indians were included among those to benefit from iron products from the Ironworks. . . . As a matter of interest, the famous iron tomahawk snatched by Hannah Dustin in March 1697 from her Indian captor while he slept, and with which she killed all ten Indians who were asleep in the wigwam, escaping with their scalps, is nearly identical to the Hammersmith specimen."

Fowler then pointed out that the Saugus finds supported his previously published contention that "all during the seventeenth century metal hatchets that found their way into Indian hands probably were plainly constructed small axes for the most part. . . . It is altogether possible that the Dustin tomahawk of 1697 is a Saugus product that found its way into Indian hands years before it turned up in such a spectacular way."

In his report Fowler cited my discovery of a land deed of 1677 in which one hundred jew's-harps and one hundred and twenty pipes were given as payment for a sizable tract of Indian domain. Never famous for developing their own instruments, the aborigines apparently had found undreamed of pleasure in the miniature lyres that brought forth tunes when held to the mouth and stroked.

To show how the Saugus evidence helps to date artifacts recovered from Indian camps or graves, Fowler compared a Saugus white-clay pipe with one found in an excavation near Churchill Lake, Maine, thus associating one more Indian encampment with the seventeenth century. Fowler concluded that brass pins we found had been made not only for domestic consumption but for trade with the natives as well. "Hand made silver pins akin to these brass ones in head style were recovered from the Fort Hill Indian stockade in North Middleboro, Massachusetts, by the Cohannet Chapter of the Society. In fact," he summed up, "all remaining kinds of objects may likewise have served as trade

Pipe Hunting, Potsherds, Arrowheads, Artifacts

229

goods at one time or another and may be expected to appear from time to time at Indian habitation sites."

Archaeologists are constantly interdependent—especially in the interpretation of artifacts. From the earliest days at Saugus, I have been seemingly pursued by clay-pipe fragments, which sometimes litter the soil as abundantly as pebbles. Not long ago I found more than 5,000 in one small area scarcely twenty-five feet square. In these encounters I have turned to a colleague who for a score of years has been tracing the chronology of clay pipes throughout the world. Geiger Omwake and others like him have become specialists upon whom excavators can depend when clay pipe artifacts are important in narrowing the chronological focus of the site. Many pipes bear a touchmark and the initials of the maker; for instance, we can trace the trade routes of Robert Tippet from his factory in Bristol, England, to diverse points in America—in my own experience, from Saugus to Tarrytown.

At Saugus we found spoons covered with a thin layer of brass which, when examined by C. Malcolm Watkins of the Smithsonian Institution, were interpreted as evidence of a period of experiment at the Jenks works, a heretofore undiscovered chapter in the history of Massachusetts craftsmanship. One of our rarest finds was a pewter nipple, a hardy reminder of days when comfort, even for babies, was limited. Aside from William Curtis's toolmaking die, we found part of a die for cutting threads on metal, seventeenth-century calipers, scissors, tongs, breach plugs and parts of barrels of early guns manufactured by Joseph Jenks; there were saws, files, shoes for horses and oxen, wrought-iron hardware, kettles with five-sided legs—all items which give us a glimpse into the everyday life of the early settlers in New England.

Many of these things had no recognizable surfaces when our shovels brought them to light. Such objects of iron and steel present perhaps the most intractable of restoration problems because

Well-preserved cutlass was found in a clay pit at Jamestown.

Heavy siege helmet, weighing more than eight pounds, was found at Jamestown in 1953 by Sergeant Floyd E. Painter.

Large German stoneware jug unearthed at Jamestown bears the date 1661. The face on the neck is remarkably similar to the face on the Bellarmine jug found at Philipsburg Manor.

Giant Saugus hammer head as it appeared after soil was removed.

of the variety and complexity of corrosions. Metals are seldom found in uncontaminated condition; they occur in combination with non-metallic elements in the form of minerals from which the workable metal must be separated by smelting. Reversing the process, buried iron products tend to return to a mineral condition, absorbing the other elements that surround them in the earth. The rate of corrosion is governed by the degree of acidity in the soil, its porosity, and the presence of natural soluble salts.

Buried for generations, an object as simple as a horseshoe begins to lose its man-made shape when oxygen, in the presence of moisture, forms rust, the characteristic orange and red compounds that are the first products of corrosion. These appear initially as a mixture of ferrous and ferric hydroxides, and progress to a stage in which some carbonate complicates the condition. Salts that can act as electrolytes increase the corrosion—until the shape of the horseshoe has vanished and the object seems as mysterious as a fragment of a meteorite.

Needless to say there is no single road to success in trying to restore and preserve metal artifacts. At Saugus, after various experiments, most of the iron relics were cleaned with disc velocity brushes, utilizing the brass wire rotary type powered by a small electric motor; some of these brushes were so soft they didn't damage the skin when accidental contact was made, yet they quickly reduced centuries of encrustations. For iron found in wet soil, I prepared a bath of fifty per cent raw linseed oil and fifty per cent range oil, seeing to it that the artifact was submerged immediately. As a rule, one or two days in the mixture softened the collected rust so that gentle tapping with the edge of a chisel, or a similar tool, would break it loose; tools discarded by my dentist also proved of great service.

With objects to which rust clings tenaciously, one of the accepted methods is the use of electrolysis. In a glass container filled with a 2.5 per cent caustic soda solution, the artifact is suspended

Pipe Hunting, Potsherds, Arrowheads, Artifacts

233

on a copper wire attached to the negative pole of a battery; a piece of graphite is wired to the positive pole and dropped into the solution. Thus an electric current passes through the artifact and combines with the caustic solution to remove the encrustation. When relics are too frail for electrolytic reduction, they are sometimes boiled in several lots of diluted caustic soda solution, then boiled again several times in distilled water.

At Philipsburg Manor we dipped copper and brass pieces in muriatic acid. These pieces were first washed and cleaned and then soaked—large pieces in undiluted acid, small objects like buttons and buckles in acid mixed with water. After a piece developed a coating, usually grayish white, it was rubbed down with steel wool under hot running water. Cold water will also work, but not as efficiently. The objects were buffed with a steel brush, then with a pad. They were coated with silver polish and shined, and washed again to remove the greasy film of the polish. Finally a coating of clear lacquer was applied.

It is unusual to find wooden artifacts simply because wood normally decays under combined biological and chemical attack from underground sources. It is common in the United States to find a dark discoloration in the soil that defines the location of a post which has decayed or—as I found at Saugus—the larger circle of an anvil base. The excavators of the burial ship found at Sutton Hoo in Suffolk, England, uncovered only stained impressions in the sand to mark where the wooden vessel had rested. More often than not, wood deteriorates so completely that nothing remains but soil of a different color and chemical content. In exceptional circumstances, however, wood has been found to survive prolonged exposure to extremes of dryness or wetness. Timbers found in dry Egyptian tombs are still as sound as when they were interred in the days of the early dynasties. And wood buried in wet peat bogs, where the absence of oxygen inhibits fungoid attacks, maintains its shape for centuries—only to disintegrate when exposed to air.

Heavy encrustation on pot found at Saugus was caused by centuries of burial.

Some machinery parts unearthed at Saugus were almost unrecognizable as the result of corrosion.

It is easy enough to preserve waterlogged wood by pickling it in a solution of water and disinfectant, but many experiments have been tried in the effort to preserve pieces so large that an air-tight container was impractical. The famous Viking ships, found buried in blue clay and now on display in Oslo, were subjected to a method in which wood is submerged in a hot bath containing potash alum and glycerine at a temperature of 92-96° C., for from ten to thirty hours. When the wood dried it was coated with equal parts of linseed oil and turpentine.

In addition to the vat we used at Saugus, I called on my experience in painting houses to devise a method that eliminated the need for a container commodious enough for large pieces. As soon as the surface of the wood began to dry but before it began to contract, we brushed on a mixture of equal parts of floor oil and substitute turpentine, applying it freely. This didn't seal the interior moisture, which continued its slow drying. As the surface became pliable, and as long as the grain absorbed the mixture, the application was continued. After several weeks, when absorption was very slow, I applied one hundred per cent floor oil. Once the wood had been dehydrated and had absorbed all the floor oil it could hold, the remainder could be easily wiped off, and the timbers took on a natural aged appearance.

Because I have done considerable digging in tidal areas and beside running streams, I've found that Nature has been generous in preserving many important wooden trophies of our past. Yet it is pottery, in the form of sherds or broken pieces, that is more readily found by the average historic-sites archaeologist. Potsherds are always valuable to the digger as a ready key to chronology. They have been termed the alphabet of archaeology. They help to define and relate time periods in prehistory and to amplify our knowledge of specific dates on historical excavations. And potsherds help us to dig up people, for the skill with which the pottery has been made, the artistry of its design, reflects not only technology but taste. Man has made containers for his food since he boiled his first stew in animal skin, but his evolution toward gracious living began, perhaps, with his discovery of ceramics which gave him a chance to express his choice of design and color. Since then, by carelessly burying broken pieces, he has left a record of developing taste which, more often than not, remains haphazard until archaeology steps in.

As a matter of fact it isn't very long since historians were mistakenly convinced that delftware—to cite one type of pottery known in Colonial America—was imported only by aristocrats, that it was never used on "plebeian tables." Digging has discharged that rather snobbish myth, for delft sherds have been found in abundance at sites occupied by families in almost every walk of life. At site after site in Jamestown—although there was a local potter to make utilitarian earthenware—the great majority of sherds were from imported English delft, slipware (the primitive clay-glazed pottery), *maiolica* from Italy, and salt-glazed ware from Germany. Conversely, at Tarrytown, pottery experts were surprised to find, at this country seat of a man of noble station, so little delft and so much common slipware.

All pottery fragments should be collected from any site, although experience will soon lead the digger to put aside the obvious chaff. Final classification must be left to experts. Meanwhile, each piece should be washed and marked with an indication of the site, the area, square or trench involved, as well as the layer of the stratification, when pertinent. When piecing-together is attempted, the simplest method is to put rims, bases and plain sherds in separate lots. The assembly of pottery fragments is even closer to working a jigsaw puzzle than archaeology itself; it's a game that an assistant of mine insisted was only for those with special talent. Perhaps so. It does take infinite patience to put together a vase from a scattering of many irregular fragments, yet it can be fun. Almost never, though, can every single piece be found, and it is

Pipe Hunting, Potsherds, Arrowheads, Artifacts

sometimes good to fill blank spaces with plaster colored to match the original. This can be accomplished rather simply by applying on the inside of the object a quarter-inch slab of Plasticine, large enough to cover the missing piece. The mold thus formed is filled with plaster of Paris and smoothed on the outside to blend with existing contours.

Indian pottery is frequently inadequately baked; it is soft and porous as a result, and very frail in wet conditions. When such pieces are found, the wisest thing is to expose them as much as possible to the sun and let them dry *in situ*. Washing with water should be avoided unless the artifact has been treated with nitro-cellulose.

There is a prosaic quality to run-of-the-mine Indian pottery, most of it being confined to geometric patterns either punctuated or painted in monochrome. The most interesting exception to come to my attention is the artisanship of the lost southwestern tribe now called the Mimbreños because their settlements were along the Mimbres River in southwestern New Mexico. A thousand years ago these potters were making handsomely turned bowls which they decorated with colorful scenes depicting their daily life. One showing a young couple behind a hanging blanket tells of an aboriginal form of bundling: when a betrothal was considered official, it was usual for the boy and girl to appear in public to converse together—with a blanket as a warning against eavesdroppers.

Most Indian remains speak much less entertainingly of prehistoric life, and yet they have collective value. Obvious artifacts like projectile points (whether for arrows, spears, or *atlatls*), grooved axes, celts, bone and antler awls, needles, fishhooks, shell spoons, and hoes—all of these are worthy finds for the amateur digger. A fluted piece of flint in an Ipswich gravel pit may well prove to have been chipped into a weapon by human hands as

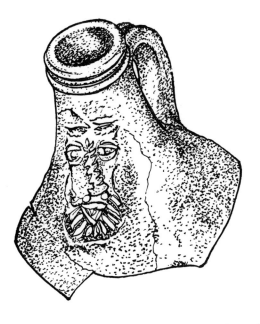

Bellarmine jug found at Philipsburg
Manor has bearded face embossed
on neck.

Broken Dutch wineglass: a clue to
domestic life at Philipsburg Manor.

Pieces of window glass and corroded nails found at the site of Thoreau's house at Walden.

Excavation of area outlined in white, on the millpond shore at Philipsburg Manor, had produced all of the artifacts piled here.

long ago as 17,000 years. It doesn't matter that its age is still at hazard. The point is that in various parts of the country men with a thirst for knowledge are giving their own time to the search for new clues. The end of the mystery may be within their sites.

In such finds there is no challenge for a "pot hunter," for a Giovanni Belzoni who, while hunting treasure, could scratch his initials in the tomb of Ramses II at Thebes. The reward for this search is fact. Through the process of compiling, exchanging data with colleagues, building a cohesive picture of migrations and habitations in a single area, fact materializes. The study of flint weapons, stone tools—our chief links with Stone Age America—and the collection of thousands upon thousands of them by organized amateurs provides the necessary material for professional conclusions.

A single site may produce chipped implements made from white quartz, felsite, shale, quartzite, chert, rhyolite, black flint, purple jasper, and agate. The lot may include as many as thirty various forms of common projectile points, a handful of drills, gouges, skin scrapers, stone sinkers, a grooved ax, an ovate knife. Each must be faithfully recorded if it is to serve anything more than a pot hunter's wanton need. There is not yet any absolute in the classification of such primitive artifacts, because new facts are continually being added to the ponderous collection of detail. Because archaeologists are aware that the shape and size of stone implements result from the limitations of available material, from the technique of manufacture, and from the use for which the implements are intended, they can only point to certain forms that appear again and again; classification is still tentative.

Perhaps surprisingly, this is not a deterrent. As an example of amateur dedication, the Washington Archaeological Society in Seattle set up a laboratory on the third floor of the home of its president, an electrical engineer. Under bright fluorescent light they placed filing-cabinets and work tables on which in one year they devoted one thousand man hours to the analysis of five hundred specimens collected at a site near the town of Vantage. Two teen-agers mimeographed a booklet of illustrated samples for use in classifying finds. With the help of a university archaeologist, each find was measured and its details recorded on a file card, and finally a sixty-four-page report, complete with photographs, was submitted to the Department of the Interior and the Smithsonian Institution in accordance with the federal antiquities act which permitted the group to dig on government land.

Why the interest in this seemingly tedious work? "Let's put it this way," one Seattle amateur said. "My great-grandparents home-

Top of Spanish olive jar found on surface of Fort Raleigh ditch.

The principal ingredient in putting together pottery pieces is patience.

steaded on Washington land that originally belonged to the Indians. The least I can do in payment is to help preserve the last remaining record of the Indian way of life."

As I've pointed out, thousands of clay pipes made for trade with the Indians have turned up in my various digs, but I haven't yet encountered any pipe of aboriginal manufacture. Archaeologists concentrating on Indians do, of course. Bill Fowler has excavated many sites to trace the evolution of pipes, turning up unfinished Stone Age pipe forms in several soapstone quarries, and following their lineage down to ceremonial iron tomahawks, one of which was found along the Damariscotta in Maine. Other pipes have been unearthed in the graves of babies, where they were left by parents who believed that the child would continue to grow in the Happy Hunting Ground, and there, when he reached manhood, the pipe would comfort him.

Pipe Hunting, Potsherds, Arrowheads, Artifacts

In Massachusetts the earliest known stone pipes were carved from soapstones such as steatite or pale-green chlorite and are found today in places where Early Man burrowed deep in cliffs to gouge out bowls and other utensils. Later he turned to sandstone and limestone as a better material for his pipes. Still later he shaped them with clay and baked them to a fine hardness along with his pottery.

Who was the genius who combined the pipe with the tomahawk? Historians believe it was a white man, and archaeology has yet to turn up contradictory evidence. Like the European clay pipe, this "smoking ax" was zestfully accepted by the natives. A broad-bladed felling-hatchet with a pipe bowl inserted in the poll can be seen in the portrait of the "Four Kings of Canada" drawn by Simon P. Verelst during the London visit of a quartet of Iroquois chiefs in 1709-10. From the Atlantic to the Rocky Mountains, Indians took to the pipe-tomahawk as an indispensable part of their war gear. "Since it served a dual purpose," says Fowler, "it lessened the encumbrances of the warrior who otherwise would have been forced to carry a separate stone or ceramic pipe."

Artifacts—the leavings of the dead? Far more than that, they speak to us of life. Corroded they may be, mouldering, broken, unfinished perhaps, sometimes cruder than their modern counterparts, seldom pretty, they live as treasure.

A glob of Massachusetts clay, hand-shaped and baked as a water-struck brick, still musty from its century in Walden earth, is now enshrined in a museum in India. Presented by the Thoreau Society to the Indian government, it bears a plaque describing it: This brick helped to build the house of Henry David Thoreau, author of *Walden* and *Civil Disobedience*, a man who inspired Mahatma Gandhi.

This—like grander things, like humbler things—is an artifact.

13

A Future for the Past

FROM A PLANE flying low over the open land, the American past is to be seen in glimpses. Shadowy outlines trace the confines of forts and villages, abandoned farms and battlegrounds. Down below, some of that past has begun to live again in the shape of restorations. The nation's first successful ironworks stands, rebuilt, at Saugus. Colonial Williamsburg thrives. An excavated earthwork fortress now is visible on the site of George Washington's first battle at Fort Necessity, south of Pittsburgh. The pioneer village of Hopewell, Pennsylvania, is restored.

Yet the view from the air shows a thousand American landmarks, grassed over, lurking among new growths of trees, sometimes visible only as a coloration in a cultivated field. No archaeologist has come near most of these, but some of them, surely, in the years ahead, will be opened up.

Some day, instead of knowing merely that Hernando de Soto marched north from Florida, then worked his way west through the Delta country, through Arkansas to Oklahoma, we may unearth the campsite where he wintered in 1541-2. Not long ago in Kansas a piece of Spanish chain mail was discovered, and at another site a sword which bears the name of an officer who set forth from Mexico with Captain-General Francisco Vasquez de Coro‑nado. Such artifacts as these may lead diggers to new details about the conquistadors. Surely there is more to learn about the Coronado stone enshrined in that glass case in Lyons, Kansas. Across that massive fragment Spanish words are chiseled:

AUGUST THE THIRD
1541
I take
for Spain
Quiver
(F)rancisco. . . .

Quivera—golden city of myth. Just as it lured Coronado, it may beckon scientists to new knowledge of the sixteenth-century middle west. And what of Drake's Bay in California where archaeologists for years have been seeking the exact site of the English landfall in 1579? Or Père Jacques Marquette's Fort Crèvecoeur erected on the wilderness shore of the Illinois River precisely a century later? The National Park Service has excavated at such similar sites as Fort Frederica in Georgia, and Fort Vancouver in Washington. More recently the Park Service joined with the American Museum of Natural History to search for the seventeenth-century redoubt built by Henri Tonti on the Arkansas River southeast of Little Rock.

Exploratory excavations have been made, too, at Crown Point, New York, where the Dutch, the English, and the French staked

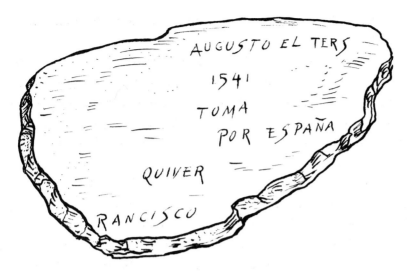

The Coronado Stone.

overlapping claims in the seventeenth and eighteenth centuries. At the head of Lake Champlain on this jut of land the French called *La Pointe de la Chevelure*—the point of scalps—stand the ruins of Fort St. Frederic, built in 1731. Near by are the broken walls of stone barracks within the giant, earthen Fort Crown Point, thrown up by Lord Jeffrey Amherst at a cost of $10,000,000. On a farm adjoining these two state-owned landmarks is the site of the French town that existed for more than a quarter-century, and was considered before the French and Indian War the most important French community south of Montreal. In *Travels in North America*, the Swedish scientist Peter Kalm tells of his visit here in 1749; he describes a thriving settlement with cultivated gardens, a church within the ramparts, and a vessel that made regular trips down Lake Champlain to St. Johns in Canada. Rogers's Rangers made one of their predatory raids here in 1756, and Robert Rogers's journal describes the prosperous Crown Point farms he burned. An end came to the French community on July 31, 1759, when—outnumbered by Amherst forces—the French troops blew

A Future for the Past

247

up Fort St. Frederic, and more than a thousand inhabitants of the near-by village fled to Canada.

This soil is so historically fertile that I am hopeful an archaeological school will be set up here to give field training to amateurs. Surveys have indicated that the area includes the sites of two outpost forts—one built by General Thomas Gage—two burying grounds, a trading-post, escape tunnels, a market place, and a lime kiln. New York teen-agers have done some digging here in recent summers under the supervision of Louis F. Ismay, the director of the Rensselaer County Junior Museum in Troy. They turned up both French and English military artifacts, and one youngster, Bernard Rottschaefer of East Greenbush, scraped out an apothecary's measure which research in London indicated had been lost

Contemporary drawing shows Fort St. Frederic just before French troops destroyed it in their retreat to Canada in 1759.

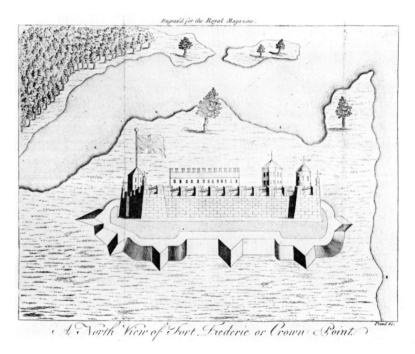

A North View of Fort Frederic or Crown Point.

Fort Crown Point as seen today from the air.

Eighteenth century map of Crown Point penninsula showing enlarged plan of English fortifications inset at right.

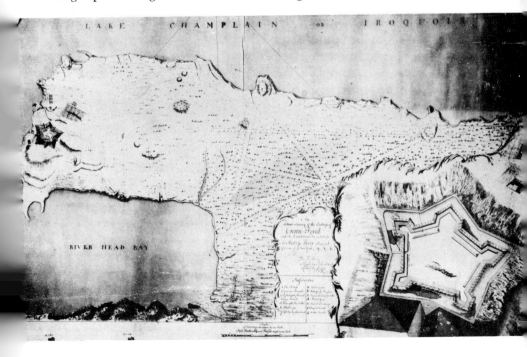

Youngsters under direction of Louis Ismay are shown digging in the area just west of the earthen ramparts at Crown Point.

when the American colonials burned the Crown Point settlement in 1776. My own preliminary digging has promised a bonanza of relics to call new attention to this historic battleground. No American landmark could serve as a better archaeological training-field than this peninsula where Samuel de Champlain defeated the Iroquois in 1609.

The remains of forts are among the most enticing targets for historic-site archaeologists. They exist wherever man has fought for his right to live. Almost invariably, they represent not one occupation but several, for even the most impregnable bastion is apt to change hands more than once. As a result, the underground story tells of the lives of men under stress, and of the military strategy and tactics they have employed in their determination to survive.

J. C. Harrington of the National Park Service has excavated a number of American forts. When he arrived in 1947 in North Carolina, at the site of Fort Raleigh and the ill-fated English colony, the history was familiar: In April 1585, Sir Richard Grenville had been sent by Sir Walter Raleigh to found a colony in the New World. In seven ships carrying one hundred and eight persons, the Grenville expedition sailed first to Puerto Rico where a fort was designed and built by Ralph Lane; then they cruised north along the mainland coast to Albemarle Sound. Settling on the island they named Roanoke, the colonists managed to stay friendly with the Indians through the winter, but trouble began in the spring. By June there was open war, ended only when the chance of escape was furnished by the fortuitous arrival of Francis Drake. With John White as governor, another group arrived in 1587, and on their second day White "walked to the North end of

Fort Raleigh at the finish of excavation and reconstruction.

the island, where Master Ralfe Lane had his forte, with sundry necessary and decent dwelling houses made by his men about it the yeere before." This was the summer Virginia Dare was born, and the year that Governor White sailed back to England to organize supplies. Delayed by the outbreak of war with Spain, White did not return to Roanoke until 1590. He found no trace of the settlers except the word CROATOAN carved on a tree, an apparent reference to a near-by island held by friendly Indians. Never again was there further news of the people who had lived beside Ralph Lane's fort.

As Harrington surveyed the twentieth-century scene he knew there were many problems. Indians had lived on the site. Confederate soldiers had been stationed here. In 1896 a man named Talcott Williams had conducted an inconclusive excavation. A magazine article describing the site in 1860 said that a "trench is clearly traceable in a square of about forty yards each way . . . another trench, perhaps flanking the gate-way, runs in some fifteen or twenty feet . . . on the right of the same face of the inclosure, the corner is apparently thrown out in the form of a small bastion. . . . A fragment or two of stone or brick may be discovered in the grass, and then all is told of the existing relics of the city of Raleigh." Eighty-seven years later, Harrington faced a site so changed that he could recognize nothing.

"The first thing we did," he told a meeting of the American Association for State and Local History, "was to excavate an exploratory trench, five feet wide, straight across one edge of the traditional fort site." Would there be anything recognizable underground? His trench cut across two ditches which, when the soils were analyzed, proved beyond doubt to be the remains of something very old—perhaps an earthwork. Still, there was no clue to

Thousands of tourists visit Fort Raleigh restoration annually.

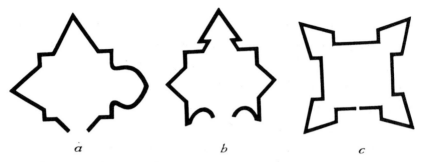

Drawings showing plan of Fort Raleigh (left) in comparison
with Ralph Lane's fort (center) and a conventional earthwork
with corner bastions.

associate the buried remains with the sixteenth century.

"The next question was to determine whether these were remains of the 1585 fort, or of a later defense work, possibly even a
Civil War fort, of which there are several nearby. . . . We recognized that the one definite means of identification would be the
finding of objects of the Elizabethan period in such a position that
their presence could only be explained by the acceptance of this
ditch as part of the original fort."

Excavating with great caution, Harrington's crew followed the
hard-packed course of the ditch. They found that wind, rain, and
snow had washed the parapet of the fort into the ditch, along with
a good deal of leaf mold which chemical analysis indicated to be
of considerable age. When they uncovered the principal entrance
to the entrenchment, it became apparent that they were indeed
exposing the eroded, long-buried fort—"for it was almost identical
to the one at Puerto Rico. Moreover, it was typically medieval in
form, especially in the absence of conventional bastions which
became so systematized and stylized in defensive works of this
nature soon after this time."

Not until 1950, however, did Harrington find the artifacts he
wanted for final proof. Embedded in the ditch surface that summer
he spotted a sixteenth-century wrought-iron sickle. Had it been

hammered out at the first forge set up by the Lost Colony's black-smith? He found three brass jettons, the device used for keeping arithmetical accounts during the sixteenth century; they carry the Tudor cross, the ironic message "True good fortune comes from God," and the name of Hans Schultes Zu Nuremberg who was known as a manufacturer of tokens from 1550 to 1574. As evidence of the colonists' sojourn in the Spanish West Indies, fragments of *maiolica* were found, as well as enough pottery pieces to form the top of a jar of the type known to have been used to contain olives.

Ralph Lane's medieval fort proved to be basically square, with pointed bastions on two sides and an octagonal bastion on the third side. Harrington's crew reconstructed it by excavating the exact shape of the ditch and repacking, in the original form, the soil of the parapets that had slipped down into the ditch. Roughly star-shaped, ready for foot soldiers to mount the firing steps and fire from the gun embrasures, it rises out of the sandy soil just as it did when the Roanoke Indians hunted in the forest and history's curtain dropped for all time on Virginia Dare and the Lost Colony.

It is a more romantic project than some, this dig for the first English structure in the United States, but the many buried forts scattered across our landscape provide opportunities for the digger no less exciting and historically valuable.

Two sides of Hans Schultes's counter found at Fort Raleigh.

A Future for the Past

In the spring and summer of 1958, five New York amateurs dug into a backyard in the Bronx and uncovered the remains of Fort Independence, built by Washington's engineers in 1776. Harry Trowbridge, Michael Cohn, Julius Lopez, Julius Diosi, and Stanley Wisniewski had been digging at Indian sites in the New York area for years, and at various times one or the other had consulted me when a colonial artifact had been found in association with aboriginal remains. The dig in the yard on 238th Street, however, was their first try at a historical site. It was made possible when a Victorian home was torn down to make way for an apartment house.

Test-trenching through the fill soils dumped here during the last hundred years, the five men struck the foundation stones of the fort's storage vault. They exposed the colonial stonework with shovels and trowels, systematically sifting the earth. Gradually, four walls, between sixteen and nineteen inches thick, came to light. They found six-pound cannon balls, and half-inch musket balls that had been squared into dice for soldierly gambling. Like Bolton and Calver before them, they turned up metal buttons bearing regimental insignia. They found the remains of rum bottles, crockery, metal tent pegs, a soldier's knife. Comparison of the data found underground with the historical descriptions of Fort Independence indicated that they had unearthed the powder magazine and officer's headquarters. The site is not spectacular enough to be preserved in the face of New York's restless urge to build and rebuild, but this dig by five amateurs has added new details to the story of the Revolutionary War.

Some diggers find fascination, not only in excavating forts and battlegrounds, but also in tracing military roads. The Crown Point Road Association was formed to chart the army link between Lake Champlain and the Connecticut River; more than three hundred Vermonters spent years in identifying the Hubbardton Military Road; still others long pursued the Bayley-Hazen supply route toward Canada.

Can moldering logs and wagon ruts be taken seriously as archaeological treasure? Why do so many men, women, and children respond so eagerly to antiquities which seem so unrewarding?

I have heard it said that we archaeologists are like ostriches, burying our heads in the past to avoid the menacing present. This is nonsense. Archaeology is for those who want adventure. It has the kind of appeal that makes some men want to climb mountains—and it has a different kind of challenge. Every serious digger I know feels a surge of excitement at the first hint of discovery; he can't resist the lure of the unknown, whether it turns out to be pirate's trove or a coin minted by the Republic of Vermont in the eighteenth century. The discovery needs no negotiable value; the excitement comes with the unearthing of something lost. An artifact may crumble into dust when exposed to air, but having unearthed it with a putty knife, under layers of earth on which we once walked completely oblivious of it, we are transported in imagination to that lost time when others lived upon our land and fashioned a world that, no matter how similar, is different from our own.

The National Park Service has a Historic Sites Survey to analyze archaeological potentials, assessing sites in terms of regional, state, or local significance—an obvious aid to non-professional diggers. To accept the responsibility for local projects, more and more amateur groups have been organized. Most of them are leagued together in state associations, a score of which are members of the Eastern States Archaeological Federation. Many other non-professionals are active in the Society for American Archaeology. The value of these groups is difficult to exaggerate, for their effect is to pool the efforts of individual diggers and to sharpen their talents so successfully that tightly disciplined amateur teams not infrequently perform excavations that might do credit to the professional. And, at last, credit has come to the unpaid digger.

To cite the words of William A. Ritchie, state archaeologist for

A Future for the Past

Vermont copper penny minted by Reuben Harmon.

New York: "There is much need for the amateur in the search for the means of obtaining a broader and deeper perspective of man's past achievements. . . . The amateur can participate in this quest fruitfully and with immense self-satisfaction; his rewards here far transcend the possession of a collection of mute relics. When once he senses the pursuit of a problem, his mind will kindle to new and exciting adventures beyond the ordinary thrill of collecting. He can have his holiday with its relaxation, anticipation, and the thrill of discovery."

Ritchie, and other state archaeologists, delegate much of their time to visiting sites opened up by amateurs in the effort to increase the public value of the digging done by non-professionals. Each of the organized societies is actively campaigning for new members—and working militantly for the appointment of a state archaeologist in each state where none exists. Construction programs, slicing through the earth in the interest of twentieth-century efficiency, are not designed to ponder over the middens of other centuries, and the consequent destruction of buried relics brings a sense of urgency to all who would find and identify the history that is still interred.

Gladys D. Weinberg, editor of the quarterly magazine of the Archaeological Institute of America, points up this fact: "The Missouri Archaeological Society—which I believe is one of the largest, if not the largest of all—has nearly 1,300 members, many of whom get up at four or five a.m. on Sunday mornings to drive a couple of hundred miles to take part in an excavation supervised by professionals. Nobody who has seen these businessmen, farmers and housewives literally on their knees, scraping away at prehistoric stratum, could doubt the enthusiasm of amateurs."

Not surprisingly, it was amateur enthusiasm as long ago as 1572 that sparked the formation of the first archaeological society under the leadership of Archbishop Matthew Parker of London. Though James I, accusing these antiquarians of political rather than scholarly motives, abolished the group, it was revived in 1707 and exists today as one of the world's most distinguished learned societies. In the United States a similar organization was tried in 1845, but it failed because there was so little interest then in the American Indian. Not until 1879 was the Archaeological Institute of America organized, and it was 1935 before the Society for American Archaeology took shape. These are parent groups with local chapters scattered throughout the country and with an increasing percentage of non-professionals as members. They form the network of scholarship that holds together all serious archaeological projects, but the yeoman service in the field is performed by those who thirst for action, the members of local and state societies. There are still hobbyists who collect clay pipes and arrowheads, just as one man collects coins and another stamps, but the dedicated and intelligent amateur archaeologist is not so easily content.

"The spade of the archaeologist, correcting and enlarging the study of historians, the discovery and scrutiny of excavations, ruins, stones, inscriptions, coins, and skeletons," wrote Sir Winston Churchill, "are telling a tale which none can doubt."

Nor is there the slightest doubt about the wonders of the tale that archaeology tells—and, fortunately for us, these wonders are virtually inexhaustable. In this country, where the study of the past remains so new, more and more of us will be digging for generations to come.

Reading List

Atkinson, R. F. C.: *Field Archaeology*. Second edition, London: Methuen & Co.; 1953. Detailed guidance.

Bibby, Geoffrey: *The Testimony of the Spade*. New York: Alfred A. Knopf; 1956.

Calver, William L. and Reginald Bolton: *History Written with Pick and Shovel*. New York: New-York Historical Society; 1950. Compiled reports of excavations by the Field Exploration Committee of The New-York Historical Society.

Ceram, C. W.: *Gods, Graves, and Scholars*. New York: Alfred A. Knopf; 1951. The account of the explorations of great archaeologists, from Schliemann to Thompson's discovery of Chichen-Itza.

Ceram, C. W.: *The March of Archaeology*. New York: Alfred A. Knopf; 1958. The story of archaeology in text and pictures.

Ceram, C. W.: *The Secret of the Hittites*. New York: Alfred A. Knopf; 1956.

Childe, V. Gordon: *The Dawn of European Civilization.* New York: Alfred A. Knopf; 1958.

Childe, V. Gordon: *Piecing Together the Past.* New York: Alfred A. Knopf; 1956.

Cookson, M. B.: *Photography for Archaeologists.* London: Max Parrish & Co.; 1954.

Coon, Carleton S.: *The Seven Caves.* New York: Alfred A. Knopf; 1957. Archaeological explorations in the Middle East.

Coon, Carleton S.: *The Story of Man.* New York: Alfred A. Knopf; 1954.

Cotter, John L. and John M. Corbett: *Archeology of the Bynum Mounds.* Washington, D.C.: Government Printing Office; 1951. Report of excavations in Northeastern Mississippi.

Cotter, John L. and Paul M. Hudson: *New Discoveries at Jamestown.* Washington, D.C.: Government Printing Office; 1957.

Fairbanks, Charles H.: *Archeology of the Funeral Mounds, Ocmulgee.* Washington, D.C.: Government Printing Office; 1956.

Frantz, Alison: "Truth Before Beauty, or, the Incompleat Photographer." *Archaeology,* Vol. III, No. 4 (Winter 1950).

Griffin, James B.: *Archaeology in the Eastern United States.* Chicago: University of Chicago Press; 1952. Comprehensive survey of American Indian archaeology.

Hartley, E. N.: *Ironworks on the Saugus.* Stillwater, Oklahoma: University of Oklahoma Press; 1957. Detailed history of Saugus ironworks based on archaeological as well as archive research.

Hatch, Charles E., Jr.: *Jamestown, Virginia, the Townsite and Its Story.* Washington, D.C.: Government Printing Office; 1957.

Heizer, Robert F.: *A Manual of Archaeological Field Methods.* Palo Alto, California: The National Press; 1956.

Heyerdahl, Thor: *Aku Aku.* Chicago: Rand McNally & Co.; 1958. Excavations on Easter Island.

Hibben, Frank C.: *The Lost Americans.* New York: T. Y. Crowell; 1946. The explorer of Sandia Cave tells of his discovery of what he believes are traces of the "first Americans."

Holand, Hjalmar R.: *Explorations in America Before Columbus.* New York: Twayne Publishers; 1956.

Kenyon, Kathleen M.: *Beginning in Archaeology*. Revised edition; with sections on American archaeology by Saul S. Weinberg and Gladys D. Weinberg. New York: Frederick A. Praeger; 1953.

Lancaster, Pinckley, Van Cleave, and Watson: *Archaeological Excavations in Mesa Verde*. Washington, D.C.: Government Printing Office; 1954.

Morison, Samuel Eliot: *Portuguese Voyages to America in the Fifteenth Century*. Cambridge, Mass.: Harvard University Press; 1940.

Perry, Clay: *New England's Buried Treasure*. New York: Stephen Daye Press; 1946.

Petrie, W. M. Flinders: *Methods and Aims in Archaeology*. London: Macmillan and Co.; 1904.

Pohl, Frederick J.: *The Lost Discovery*. New York: W. W. Norton and Co.; 1952. An account of Vikings in America.

Pohl, Frederick J.: *The Vikings on Cape Cod*. Pictou, Nova Scotia: Advocate Press; 1957.

Radin, Paul: *The Story of the American Indian*. New York: Liveright Publishing Corp.; 1944.

Reed, Eric: "Summary of Historic Sites." *American Antiquity*, Vol. XVII (July 1951), pp. 78-81; Vol. XVIII (January 1953), pp. 287-8.

Wedel, Waldo R.: *Prehistory and the Missouri Valley Development Program*. Washington, D.C.: Smithsonian Miscellaneous Collections; 1948. Vol. v. III, No. 2. Summary report on Missouri River Basin Archaeological Survey.

Wendorf, Krieger, and Albritton: *The Midland Discovery*. Austin, Texas: University of Texas Press; 1957. The story of discovery of prehistoric human bones near Midland, Texas.

Wertenbaker, T. J.: "The Archeology of Colonial Williamsburg." *Annual Report of the Smithsonian Institution for 1953*, pp. 447-54.

Wheeler, Mortimer: *Archaeology from the Earth*. Baltimore: Penguin Books; 1956. Methods used by some archaeologists.

Wheeler, Mortimer: *Still Digging*. London: Michael Joseph; 1955.

Reading List

Woolley, Leonard: *Digging Up the Past.* Baltimore: Penguin Books; 1956. An introduction to archaeology.

Woolley, Leonard: *A Forgotten Kingdom.* Baltimore: Penguin Books; 1953. Detailed account of excavations in the Turkish Hatay.

Zeuner, F. E.: *Dating the Past.* London: Longmans, Green; 1950.

Index

INDEX

ii

INDEX

v

INDEX

Thorfinn Karlsefni, 134, 148, 149
Tide, effect of, 110, 114, 127, 149, 236
Tonti, Henri, 246
Tools, survey, 214; excavation, 215–6
Top soil, buried, 166
Travels in North America (Kalm), 247
Triangulation, 206
Trowbridge, Harry, 256
Troy, Asia Minor, 72
Troy, N. Y., 248
Truro, Mass., 4
Trustees of Public Reservations, 139
Tuckahoe plantation, 82; house described, 83
Turpentine and floor oil, use of, 236
Tyre and Judah, 147

Uhlig, Henry, 54, 55
Unit-level method, 209
University Museum of Archaeology and Ethnology, Cambridge, England, 146
University of London Institute of Archaeology, 71
University of South Dakota, 204
Upton, Mass., 139–40
Ur, 15, 210

Valley of the Kings, 223
Vantage, Wash., 242
Vassell, John, 161
Verelst, Simon P., 244
Vermont, human hibernation, 14
Vermont, Republic of, 257
Vermont Life, 141
Vescelius, Gary, 143, 145
Vesuvius, 116
Viking ships, 58, 131, 236; described, 124; Gokstad, 58, 130
Viking Ships, The (Brogger), 130
Vikings, 4, 15, 121–31, 134, 151
Vinland, 134, 148, 151, 153
Virginia, first accurate map of, 83
Voyageurs, 4, 195

Walden, 15-35, 39, 50, 197, 200, 204, 220; cairn at, 18, 19–20, 21, 25;

chimney base found, 31-2, marked, 35; Edmund Stuart Hotham at, 28
Walden (Thoreau), 18, 22–5; *quoted*, 20, 21, 22, 23, 24, 27, 28, 33, 34, 35
Washington Archaeological Society, 241
Water-pumping, 49, 56, 105, 107
Water table, 49, 51, 55, 57, 63, 80, 107, 129, 169
Water wheels, 39, 53, 58, 61, 114, 121, 172, 218; excavation of, 55–7
Watkins, C. Malcolm, 230
Webb, Dr. Thomas H., 151
Weinberg, Gladys D., *quoted*, 258–9
Wendorf, Dr. Fred, 212
Wertenbaker, Thomas Jefferson, *quoted*, 172–3
Westchester County, 98, 104
Westford, Mass., 145, 147
West Point, 7
West Quincy, Mass., 46, 50, 67, 69
Wharton Tract, N. J., 197
Wheeler, Mortimer, 70; *quoted*, 72, 210–11
Wheeler, R. G., 102, 105, 106, 160, 165
White, Gov. John, 251, 253
William III, 160; and Mary, 93
Williams, Talcot, 253
Williamsburg, 9, 10, 102–3, 245
Wilmington, N. C., 160
Winthrop, John, Jr., 46, 67, 68, 163, 228
Wisniewski, Stanley, 256
Wood, conditions under which it decays, 234; deterioration of, 129; pickling of, 236; preservation at Saugus, 58–9, 236; waterlogged, 236
Woodbury escape tunnel, 166–70; letters on, 168
Woolley, Leonard, *quoted*, 15, 203, 218

Yankee Magazine, 150; *quoted*, 150–51
Yeamans, John, 161

Zeno, Nicolo and Antonio, 146
Zurhorst, Charles, family, 158–9

A NOTE ABOUT THE AUTHORS

ROLAND WELLS ROBBINS was born in Worcester, Mass., in 1908. He left high school after his freshman year and, after a period as an office worker, set up a successful house-painting and window-washing business in Lincoln, Mass. In the early 1940's he began to make a hobby of digging for buried facts of local history; but the hobby soon became a full-time occupation and, within a few years and through intensive self-training, he had established himself as one of the country's leading professional archaeologists specializing in the discovery of historic sites. Mr. Robbins, who is married and has three children, makes his home in Lincoln when he is not traveling about the country on archaeological surveys and digs.

EVAN JONES was born in Le Sueur, Minnesota, in 1915. Educated in the public schools, he began work as a journalist while still a student. After gaining experience on newspapers in St. Paul, Minneapolis, and Chicago, Mr. Jones was editor of the magazine, *Weekend,* published for Americans abroad in Frankfurt and Paris from 1945 to 1949. Now a free-lance writer, he has written—on food, amateur archaeology, and various other subjects—for such magazines as *Look, Harper's Bazaar, Sports Illustrated, Good Housekeping,* and *The New York Time Magazine.* His article about Roland Robbins's work entitled "Pick-and-Shovel Historian," in the August 5, 1955 issue of Collier's Magazine led to their collaboration on *Hidden America.*

A NOTE ON THE TYPE AND PRODUCTION

The text of this book is set in Caledonia, a Linotype face designed by W. A. Dwiggins (1880–1956), who was responsible for so much that is good in contemporary book design. Though much of his early work was in advertising and he was the author of the standard volume Layout in Advertising, *Mr. Dwiggins later devoted his prolific talents to book typography and type design, and worked with great distinction in both fields. In addition to his designs for Caledonia, he created the Metro, Electra, and Eldorado series of type faces, as well as a number of experimental cuttings that have never been issued commercially.*

Caledonia belongs to the family of printing types called "modern face" by printers—a term used to mark the change in style of typeletters that occurred at the end of the eighteenth century. It is best evidenced in the letter shapes designed by Baskerville, Martin, Bodoni, and the Didots.

This book was composed by Howard O. Bullard Inc., New York, printed by The Murray Printing Company, Forge Village, Massachusetts, and bound by H. Wolff, New York. Designed by Guy Fleming.